P9-DWJ-048

Raymond E. Brown, S.S.

Com OJS.
mento Park
CA

A Once-and-Coming Spirit at Pentecost

Essays on the Liturgical Readings
Between Easter and Pentecost,
Taken from the Acts of the Apostles
and from the Gospel According to John

A Liturgical Press Book

The Liturgical Press
Collegeville, Minnesota

Cover design by Mary Jo Pauly

Nihil obstat: Robert C. Harren, *Censor deputatus*
Imprimatur: ✚ Jerome Hanus, O.S.B., Bishop of St. Cloud
Date: August 31, 1993

© 1994 by The Order of St. Benedict, Inc., Collegeville, Minnesota. All rights reserved. No part of this book may be reproduced in any form or by any means, electronic or mechanical, including photocopying, recording, taping, or any retrieval system, without the written permission of The Liturgical Press, Collegeville, Minnesota 56321. Printed in the United States of America.

1   2   3   4   5   6   7   8

Library of Congress Cataloging-in-Publication Data
Brown, Raymond Edward.
    A once-and-coming Spirit at Pentecost : essays on the liturgical readings between Easter and Pentecost, taken from the Acts of the Apostles and from the Gospel according to John / Raymond E. Brown.
        p.   cm.
    Includes bibliographical references.
    ISBN 0-8146-2154-6
    1. Holy Spirit—Biblical teaching. 2. Bible. N.T. Acts-
-Criticism, interpretation, etc. 3. Bible. N.T. John—Criticism,
interpretation, etc. 4. Eastertide—Liturgy. 5. Catholic Church-
-Liturgy. I. Title.
BS2625.6.H62B76   1994
226.5'06—dc20   93-28726
                                                               CIP

Foreword

Comparable in scope and format to this book, The Liturgical Press has published four volumes of my biblical reflections on Gospel passages used by the Church respectively in the liturgies of Advent, Christmas, Holy Week, and Easter. In the great liturgical cycle of salvation history from the coming of Jesus Christ to the coming of the Holy Spirit, we now come to the fifth and final liturgical period, namely, the season between Easter and Pentecost. During this season at the eucharistic liturgy the church reads from the Acts of the Apostles recounting the external life of the early Christian community *once* the Spirit had come at Pentecost, and reads from John's Gospel words of Jesus portraying the internal life of the Christian disciple and promising a *coming* Paraclete to be sent by the Father. No better guidance can be found for our own quest to be Christians living externally in a church responsive to the vagaries of history and internally as branches attached to Jesus the vine.

In 1991 Iona College in New Rochelle, New York, administered by the (Irish) Christian Brothers (C.F.C.), graciously granted me a Doctorate of Letters. I wish to express my gratitude to the Brothers for that honorary degree, and for the hospitality they have shown me in various parts of the world as far apart as Sydney and Perth in Australia and Antigua in the Caribbean. But most especially through this book I wish to thank them for eleven years of quality Christian primary and secondary education that I received at All Hallows School in New York City. My love for teaching is in no small part due to the gifted and devoted Christian Brothers who taught me.

Contents

Introduction Explaining This Treatment of the Liturgical Season

For several reasons the season between Easter and Pentecost is more complex than the other liturgical seasons on which I have reflected. I have listed the Sunday and weekday liturgical readings of this prePentecost season at the back of the book; it may be helpful to consult those lists as I discuss the complexities.

The only consistent readings for this seven-week period are from the Acts of the Apostles (beginning with 2:14), which supplies the pericopes for the first reading of the weekday and Sunday Masses. The weekday selections constitute the longest sequential reading in the Mass Lectionary from any book of the Bible outside the Gospels. Yet there is an apparent illogicality in this arrangement: The coming of the Spirit is described in Acts 2:1-11 (the passage read on the feast of Pentecost), and yet the rest of Acts is read before and not after Pentecost. Thus in the liturgical period when we are readying ourselves for the coming of the Spirit, we read what happened in the early church once the Spirit had come!

The weekday readings from the Acts of the Apostles (henceforth simply called Acts) are perfectly sequential, running from chapter 2 to the end (chapter 28).[1] Yet the selections are not proportionately distributed throughout Acts, for there is a clear bias toward the earlier part of the book. Of the forty-two weekday readings only the last three are taken from the final one-quarter of Acts (following 21:15) when Paul is seized and tried in Jerusalem and Caesarea and then sent

---

[1] The sequence is broken only on Ascension Thursday; on that feast (in some regions celebrated on Sunday) the first reading is the account of the ascension in Acts 1:1-11, and the Gospel reading is from the conclusion of Matt (A year), of Mark (B), or of Luke (C).

Introduction: Liturgical Treatment of the Readings

1

to Rome. By comparison fourteen readings are taken from the first quarter of Acts (chapters 2 through 7) describing the life of the church in Jerusalem up to the stoning of Stephen.[2] Thus there is far greater emphasis on the history of the first Christian community rather than on the career *per se* of the great apostle. True, nineteen readings are taken from the section of Acts that concern the missionary travels of Paul from the time he sets out from Antioch until he returns to Jerusalem to be arrested (13:4–21:15). Yet even in those the selection shows a minimum interest in the travels and a maximum interest in what happened in the communities that Paul converted. Thus it is fair to say that in the readings from Acts on weekdays between Easter and Pentecost the emphasis is on the life-story of the early church, Jewish (Jerusalem) and Gentile (Antioch and Pauline)—a life-story the beginnings of which will be described on Pentecost.

In the previous volumes I commented on the Gospel passages of the various seasons, but they are more complex here. The weekday Gospel readings of the 1st Week after Easter (the octave) recount the appearances of the risen Jesus, and I have already made them the subject of reflection in *A Risen Christ at Eastertime,* the fourth volume in this series. For the weekdays after Easter from the 2d Week on, the Church reads sequentially from the Gospel according to John, beginning with chapter 3. Yet there are large gaps as the Lectionary skips from chapter 3 to 6 to 10 (dialogue with Nicodemus, multiplication of the loaves, Good Shepherd, etc.) with the longest and most sequential set of readings (nineteen) devoted to the Last Supper (chapters 13–17). From a strictly exegetical viewpoint it would be difficult to write detailed sequential reflections on such selections unless one chose to ignore all the intervening material. Moreover, I have

---

[2] Or, to count in another way, eleven readings are taken from the first four chapters (2 through 5); two readings are taken from the last four chapters (25 through 28).

Introduction: Liturgical Treatment of the Readings

already written for The Liturgical Press *The Gospel and Epistles of John—A Concise Commentary,* and it would be of little interest simply to excise from that. As will become apparent, however, I shall not ignore the Gospel readings from John, even though my primary concentration will be on Acts. Just as there was an apparent illogicality in reading in this prePentecost season selections from Acts that in the storyline follow the original Pentecost, so also there is an apparent illogicality in reading in this postEaster season Johannine selections that in the storyline precede Jesus' death. Yet it is at the Last Supper that the Johannine Jesus speaks of the coming of the Paraclete.

I have been speaking about weekday readings. Would it not be of more help if I concentrated on Sunday readings? Since most clergy give brief homilies at weekday Masses, I am not sure that concentration on Sundays would be more helpful to them. But there is another reason why it may be more helpful to laity and clergy alike to concentrate on the weekday cycle as a way of making the Sunday readings intelligible. (What follows is a bit complicated; please keep an eye on the lists at the back of this book.) In this season the Sunday readings are also from Acts and John although, of course, since there are fewer Sunday readings, the selection is more limited.[3] In a certain sense the Sunday readings are a pale reflection of the wealth of the weekday readings.

Let me illustrate that claim. In any given year only five selections from Acts are read on the Sundays between Easter and Ascension. If one surveys the fifteen passages from Acts

---

[3] I refer to the first and third readings of each Sunday Mass. A glance at the first list in the back of this book will show that the Sunday readings from Acts and John are sequential from the 3rd Sunday on, but only within the given year (A, B, or C). A special case is presented by the Acts readings 1:12-14 and 1:15-17, 20-26 (A and B) of the last Sunday after Easter which are chosen as a sequence to Ascension Thursday. I remind readers that in *A Risen Christ at Eastertime* I treated the appearance of the Lord in Acts 1:1-12, which includes the ascension.

Introduction: Liturgical Treatment of the Readings

read in the course of three-year cycle of Sundays, relatively few are not included in the forty-two weekday selections that are read every year.[4] As for Gospel readings, because the first two Sundays always recount resurrection appearances, in any given year only four selections from the John's account of the public ministry of Jesus are read on the Sundays between Easter and Pentecost. If one surveys the twelve passages from John read in the course of the three-year cycle of Sundays, really only two are not included in the thirty-six weekday selections that are read every year.[5] Thus if I reflect on the weekday readings, I shall for all practical purposes have covered the Sunday readings, no matter which of the three liturgical years (A, B, C) it happens to be. Since my chapters, like the weekday order, will be strictly sequential, those who are interested primarily in a given Sunday's readings need only to look at headings of the chapters to find where that particular pericope is discussed (within the larger context that would be necessary for intelligibility in any case).

Despite the apparent illogicalities I have mentioned above, theological reflection enables us to see that there really is good sense in the Lectionary pattern of reading from Acts and John at this season. Let me explain this first in relation to the readings from Acts that describe the aftermath of the gift of the Spirit. The mystery of the resurrection that we celebrate on Easter is complex. In one action that goes beyond earthly time Jesus is victorious over death, emerges from the tomb, returns to his Father, and gives the Spirit to those who believe in him. From the viewpoint of the first followers who continued to live on within time these actions were spread out: They found the tomb empty on Sunday morning; the risen Lord appeared to them on that day or

---

[4] Namely, Acts 2:42-47 (A: 2d Sunday); 5:12-16 (C: 2d Sunday); 8:14-17 (A: 6th Sunday); 9:26-31 (B: 5th Sunday); 10:25-48 (B: 6th Sunday).

[5] Namely, John 13:31-33a, 34-35 (C: 5th Sunday), and 14:15-21 (A: 5th Sunday). Notice how the John readings of the 4th Sunday, 10:1-11 (A) and 10:11-18 (B), are dealt with on Monday of the 4th Week.

Introduction: Liturgical Treatment of the Readings

subsequently; the termination of the appearances caused them to realize that Jesus was now permanently with God; and they received the Spirit. Yet the timeless character from God's viewpoint has left its mark in the NT reports, for without embarrassment the same event is described as having taken place at different times. If one reads Hebrews 9:11-28, one gets the impression that Jesus ascended from the cross with his blood directly into heaven, even as Luke 23:43 has the dying Christ say on Good Friday, "*This day* you will be with me in Paradise." According to John 20:17 ("I am ascending to my Father and your Father"), Jesus seems to have begun his ascent to the Father on Easter Sunday in the daytime before he appears to the disciples at night. According to Luke 24:51 he ascended on Easter Sunday night, and according to Acts 1:3, 10 he ascended some forty days after Easter. Now in all these accounts the same basic action of going to God's presence, terminating Jesus' existence on earth, is involved; but it is described in different ways with different theological nuances.

The same may be said of the gift of the Spirit by the victorious Jesus. Once again it is an event that surpasses time, and accordingly is described at different moments in different New Testament narratives. In John Jesus is victorious already when he is raised up on the cross (12:31-33), and before his death he has already fulfilled all things given him by God (19:28). Thus, as he dies he gives over the Spirit to the community of special disciples at the foot of the cross (19:30), and from his dead body come forth water and blood symbolizing the gift of the Spirit (19:34; 7:38-39). Yet also in John on Easter Sunday night to "the disciples" (i.e., presumably to others than those at the cross, for this group seems to include members of the Twelve) Jesus can say, "Receive the Holy Spirit" (20:22). And, of course, Acts 2:1-4 has the Spirit come in power fifty days after Easter. Given such variation it is not illogical for the Lectionary to describe immediately after Easter the life of the Christian community called into being by the

Introduction: Liturgical Treatment of the Readings

5

risen Jesus' gift of the Spirit. The Church need not wait until the feast of Pentecost when it will solemnly celebrate that gift. Theologically it knows that the gift of the Spirit is part of an Easter mystery that goes beyond time.

As we turn to the use of the Gospel of John, we must remember that all the Gospels are written from a postresurrectional viewpoint. They differ only in the extent in which the memories of the ministry have been rewritten from that vantage, ranging in the order (from the least extent to the most) Mark, Luke, Matthew, John. In the three-year cycle the Church reads from the first three of those, one Gospel per year. Thus for the most part it reads the Gospel accounts of the ministry after Pentecost. But it has chosen to read sections of John's account of the ministry every year after Easter, thus tacitly giving recognition that it is the Gospel with the most pronounced postresurrectional reinterpretation.[6] In particular, there is no theological difficulty about reading John's account of the Last Supper after Easter because Jesus' discourse recounted in that context is addressed to Christians of all times and places, i.e., those who constitute "his own." Despite the localization on the night before Jesus died, the Johannine Jesus says, "I am no longer in the world" (17:11)—a clear indication that the evangelist was writing these words from the viewpoint of a Jesus already victorious and on his way to the Father. In other words the liturgy is actually respecting the evangelist's mindset in placing Johannine material after Easter.

How is it possible to reflect on Acts and yet take cognizance of the Johannine readings? They are complementary. Acts describes the external or visible career of Christianity from the first preaching to Jews in Jerusalem until Paul arrives in Rome, the capital of the Gentile world. The proclamation about Jesus that began among Jews has its future

[6] This custom of reading portions of John after Easter is very ancient, as old as the 4th century in some liturgies.

Introduction: Liturgical Treatment of the Readings

among Gentiles: "They will listen" (28:28). The author sees the working out of the presence of the Spirit in actions of historical persons in geographically diverse places. The Gospel of John sees the working of the Spirit in the internal life of Christians. This eternal life is given in baptism (Discourse with Nicodemus in chapter 3), nourished by the food of eternal life (Bread of Life Discourse in chapter 6), and cared for by the Good Shepherd (chapter 10). The intimate words of Jesus to his own in the Last Discourse concern the love commandment, the Paraclete, union with him and the Father—in other words all the constitutive elements of that life. To simplify, although both authors believe that Christian life manifests the Spirit, the author of Acts shows the Spirit at work in the external course of history, while the author of John shows the Spirit at work in the inner existence of the disciple. In what follows I shall reflect on the story of Acts and, in lesser space, point to the complementarity of the Johannine readings.

Introduction: Liturgical Treatment of the Readings

Chapter 1

The Church Begins in Jerusalem
(Acts 2:14-41)

The first two weekday readings after Easter and the readings of the 3d and 4th Sundays of the A year are from this section of Acts that describes Peter's first sermon and the effect it produced. It is a marvelous passage with which to begin our reflections on the church that the Spirit has produced, for it is a masterful summary of Christian essentials.

Before reflecting on it, let me say a few words about the section of Acts 2 that precedes it and that constitutes the reading on Pentecost itself. The Feast of Weeks or Pentecost (so-called because it was celebrated seven weeks or fifty days after Passover) was a pilgrimage feast when pious Jews came from their homes to the Temple or central shrine in Jerusalem. The historical nucleus of what is described in Acts 2:1-13 is seemingly that on the next pilgrimage feast after Jesus' death and resurrection his Galilean disciples and his family came to Jerusalem and that, while they were there, the presence of the Spirit was charismatically manifested as they began to speak in tongues. This was seen as a sign that they should proclaim publicly what God had done in Jesus.

Acts has re-presented that nucleus with theological insight, highlighting its central place in the Christian history of salvation. In that presentation the meaning of Pentecost plays a key role. It was an agricultural feast celebrated in May or June as a way of giving thanks to God for the wheat or grain harvest; but like the other pastoral or agricultural feasts of the Jews it had acquired another meaning, recalling what God had done for the chosen people in their history.[7] The

[7] In the case of other feasts, namely Passover/Unleavened Bread and Tabernacles (Tents, Booths), the Old Testament itself records the salvific history applications, respectively the exodus and the desert wandering on the

deliverance from Egypt was commemorated at Passover. About a month and a half later in the Exodus account (19:1) of that deliverance the Israelites arrived at Sinai; and so Pentecost, occurring about a month and a half after Passover, became the commemoration of God's giving the covenant to Israel at Sinai—the moment when Israel was called to be God's own people.

In depicting God's appearance at Sinai, Exodus 19 includes thunder and smoke; and the Jewish writer Philo (contemporary with the New Testament) describes angels taking what God said to Moses on the mountain top and carrying it out on tongues to the people on the plain below. Acts, with its description of the sound of a mighty wind and tongues as of fire, echoes that imagery, and thus presents the Pentecost in Jerusalem as the renewal of God's covenant, once more calling a people to be God's own. According to Exodus, in the Sinai covenant the people who heard the invitation to be God's own and accepted it were Israelites. After Sinai in biblical language the other nations remained "no people." Acts 2:9-11, with its broad sweep from the extremities of the Roman Empire (Parthians, Medes, and Elamites) to Rome itself, describes the nationalities who at Pentecost observed and heard what was effected by the Spirit at the Jerusalem renewal of the covenant. Thus Acts anticipates the broad reach of the evangelizing that has now begun, an evangelizing that will ultimately make even the Gentiles God's own people (Acts 28:28).[8] In the Christian estimation what hap-

---

way to the Promised Land. In the Old Testament no salvific history meaning is supplied for Weeks (Pentecost), but in later rabbinical writings the meaning given above is attested. Thanks to the preChristian *Book of Jubilees* and the Dead Sea Scrolls, we now have evidence that this meaning was known in Jesus' time.

[8] A possibility is that the list describes the areas evangelized by missionaries from the Jerusalem church (as distinct from areas evangelized from other centers like Antioch, e.g., through the journeys of Paul). In Acts 2:5 Luke describes the people from these areas as devout Jews, an identification

Chapter 1: The Church Begins in Jerusalem

pened at this Pentecost is more momentous and wider-reaching than what happened at the first Pentecost at Sinai.

Reaction to the disciples who have received the Spirit speaking in tongues—ecstatic behavior that looks to observers like drunkenness—causes Peter to deliver the first Christian sermon, a sermon that Acts conceives of as the fundamental presentation of the gospel.[9]

PETER'S SERMON (ACTS 2:14-36)

Peter interprets the action of the Spirit at Pentecost as the fulfillment of the signs of the last days foretold by the prophet Joel. In the immediate context the hearers have seen some startling things (and perhaps we are to think not only of the mighty wind and tongues of fire but also of the darkening of the sun at Jesus' death [Luke 23:44]); yet it still required faith to see that Jesus had introduced the last times. That is a message throughout the New Testament and still a message today. The world around us, even in nominally Christian areas, is less and less inclined to think that Christianity proclaims anything earth-shattering. People relying on

---

that fits the pilgrimage feast context. Yet in the total context of the book, which describes the gradual extension of the mission from Jews to Gentiles, we may be meant to see here an anticipation that all from these nations (2:17: "all flesh") would be invited and accept. In the language of the letter associated with the chief apostle of the Jerusalem church, a letter addressed to people from areas listed in Acts 2:9-11, those who were once "no people" become God's people (I Peter 2:10).

[9] In these reflections I do not plan to enter into detailed issues of historicity: Did Peter actually deliver a sermon on Pentecost itself? What did he say? The sermon in Acts is obviously composed by the author of the book, but did he have a tradition about the nucleus of the apostolic preaching? The speaking in tongues should make us cautious in our judgment. At an early level or recounting, it was obviously ecstatic, whence the appearance of drunken babbling. It has been reinterpreted in Acts as speaking in other tongues or languages which are understood—a reinterpretation that has not wiped out the earlier tradition.

Peter's Sermon

physical sight are apt to question whether the coming of
Jesus really changed anything in the world since there is still
war, oppression, poverty, and suffering. Yet we Christians
still believe and proclaim that there are radical new possibilities for life that did not exist before, for "whoever calls on
the name of the Lord shall be saved" (Acts 2:21). As Jesus
himself did, the first Christian preacher challenges human
self-sufficiency with a proclamation of both the need of
God's grace and the possibility of receiving it.

Worth noting is the fact that Peter makes this proclamation
in what we would call Old Testament terms, thus affirming
the basic consistency of what God has done in Jesus Christ
with what the God of Israel did for and promised to the
people of the covenant. Long centuries after God first called
the Hebrew slaves and made them the people of Israel, their
self-understanding would be tested as to whether anything
had really changed because of that calling, especially when
they lost the land and were carried off into exile. In other
words, they lived through beforehand what has often been
the Christian experience in the centuries after Jesus. Both
they and we have had to have the vision of faith to see
God's realities in and through a history where at times God
seems to be absent. In part that is why the Old Testament
remains an essential element in Christian proclamation. It
covers not only the establishment of the covenant but the attempt to live as God's covenanted people over a millennium
of ups and downs. The New Testament alone covers too
short a period of time and is too filled with success to give
Christians the lessons the Old Testament gives. For centuries
in Roman Catholicism the Old Testament (except for verses
from the Psalms) was never read on Sundays, leaving us un-
familiar with what was taught so well there. In the aftermath
of Vatican II that defect has been corrected, and yet it is dis-
appointing how seldom the Old Testament readings are the
subject of the homily. Preachers turn too easily and quickly
to the Gospel readings for their topic, even when the very

Chapter 1: The Church Begins in Jerusalem

thing that might most challenge their audience is in the Old Testament passage!

In what follows Peter turns from the (Old Testament) Scriptures to tell what God has done in Jesus: a brief summary of his mighty works, crucifixion and resurrection, culminating in scriptural evidence that he was the Lord and Messiah (2:36). In a certain sense this concentration on christology represents a change from Jesus' own style as narrated in the first half of Luke-Acts. Although in Luke's Gospel both an angel and God testified that Jesus is the Messiah and the Son of God, and the disciples called him Lord, Jesus did not talk directly about himself. He spoke about God's kingdom and its challenge to accepted values. Nevertheless, Acts confirms the evidence of Paul that early preachers shifted the primary focus of their proclamation to Jesus himself, almost as if they could not announce the kingdom without first telling of him through whom the kingdom was made present. The fundamental gospel became centered on the christological identity of Jesus as Messiah and Son of God (see Romans 1:3-4).

I once wrote an essay suggesting that the sermons in Acts might serve as a guide to certain fundamental aspects that should be included in Christian preaching today.[10] That holds true not only for the already-mentioned insistence on the Old Testament but also for this emphasis on christology. There are many things that need to be called to people's attention (morality, social justice, family issues, etc.), but preaching is not really Christian unless it is rooted in Jesus Christ. It is discouraging to hear sermons in Christian churches where, despite the value of the message, Jesus is scarcely mentioned. In Catholic circles this should be kept in mind when preaching the difficult demands of Christian living. Psycho-

---

[10] "The Preaching Described in Acts and Early Christian Doctrinal Priorities," reprinted in my *Biblical Exegesis and Church Doctrine* (New York: Paulist, 1985), 135-46.

logically, as a matter of persuasive procedure, it may not be wise simply to root those demands in authoritative Church teaching without going the further step of showing that the Church teaching itself is rooted in what the Lord Jesus proclaimed. There are those who will simply shrug off Church teaching as a matter of opinion, but would not so easily dismiss the issue if it were shown them that Jesus Christ, the Son of God, was no less exacting than his church.

THE RESPONSE (ACTS 2:37-41)

Having presented this model of Christian preaching, Acts now dramatizes in question and answer form the fundamentals of accepting the gospel. What must be done once people believe the proclamation that God has made the crucified Jesus Lord and Messiah (2:36-37)? Peter states specific requirements and then makes a promise. The *first* demand is to ''repent.'' In the first half of Luke-Acts the public ministry of Jesus begins with John the Baptist preaching ''a baptism of repentance'' (Luke 3:3: *metanoia*); Mark 1:4 mentions the baptism of repentance in relation to John, and then (1:14-15) has Jesus come and begin preaching: ''Repent and believe in the gospel'' (see Luke 5:32). Here, then, Acts is carefully showing continuity between the beginning of the public ministry of Jesus and the beginning of the church, between the first demand of the proclamation of the kingdom and the first demand of apostolic preaching. Literally the Greek verb *metanoein* (*meta* = ''across, over''; *noein* = ''to think'') means ''to change one's mind, way of thinking, outlook.'' The traditional translation, ''to repent,'' indicates the necessity of a change of lifestyle and direction for those who are conscious of being sinners, i.e., of being turned away from God. They must turn around toward God. But the gospel is preached also to religious people who have sought to serve God. A demand to ''repent'' often will not make an impression on them; they will think of it as a demand for others

Chapter 1: The Church Begins in Jerusalem

who are just beginning. Only when it is translated literally as a demand to change one's mind will its offensiveness penetrate. Generally religious people do not like to change their minds, for they already know what God wants. (In recent Catholic life we should remember that the greatest protest about the changes introduced by Vatican Council II came from the most observant Catholics!) If we look at the public ministry, we see that rarely, if at all, was Jesus found offensive by those who are portrayed as sinners. The religious people were the ones who found him offensive, precisely because through his parables and actions he was challenging whether their views really were God's views. Sometimes when I explain this orally, I can see people nodding their heads as they think of certain religious people who need to change their minds. That is too easy: We must be convinced that *we* need to change as much as those others. Moreover, the summons to "change your minds" because the kingdom of God is at hand, although presented at the beginning of Jesus' ministry and the beginning of the apostolic mission, cannot fully be met by a once-for-all-time response. Many times in our lives we must be willing to change our minds as a new presentation of God's will confronts us. One cannot come to Christ without responding to the challenge, "Change your minds"; one cannot remain alive and fruitful in Christ without responding to the same challenge.[11]

Second, Peter demands, "Be baptized . . . for the forgiveness of your sins" (Acts 2:38b). Although John the Baptist insisted that people receive the baptism of repentance, Jesus did not; in the first three Gospels during his whole ministry he is never shown as baptizing anyone.[12] Forgiveness of sins

---

[11] See R. D. Witherup, *Conversion in the New Testament* (Zacchaeus Studies NT; Collegeville: The Liturgical Press, 1994).

[12] Once in John (3:22) he is said to baptize, but that is corrected and denied in 4:2. In a postresurrectional appearance the Matthean Jesus tells the Eleven (the Twelve minus Judas) to make disciples of all nations, baptizing them (Matt 28:19). Not only is there no reason to think that the readers of Acts

The Response

was through the power of his word. In one way Acts is showing continuity: Jesus' power over sin remains. But now it is exercised through baptism, and so in his second demand Peter goes beyond the pattern of Jesus' lifetime. The time of the church is beginning.

Baptism is looked at in different ways in the different books of the New Testament, and our theology of baptism represents an amalgamation from those different views.[13] (I shall return to that below when I discuss baptism in John 3.) Baptism as a public action is important for our reflection here: Peter is portrayed as asking people to make a visible and verifiable profession of their acceptance of Jesus. This is tantamount to asking people to "join up." For someone who would eventually be compared, rightly or wrongly, to other founders of religions, Jesus was remarkably "unorganizational." True, he is reported as calling a few people (particularly the Twelve) to leave their work and follow him, but otherwise he seems to have been content to leave without follow-up those who encountered him and were visibly moved by what he did and said. He does not try to organize them or put specific continuing demands on them. The Gospels tell us with vague generalization that they went back to their towns and villages and reported enthusiastically what they had seen and heard. But there is no evidence of their forming "Jesus groups" in his lifetime. After the resurrection, however, his followers show an instinct to gather and hold together those whom they convince about Jesus; and their demanding an identifying sign like baptism is the first step in that process of gathering. Indeed, we have little evi-

would have known Matthew's Gospel; but also, as I explained in *A Risen Christ at Eastertime* (36–37), that Matthean scene embodies the retrospective experience of the Matthean community toward the end of the 1st century.

[13] We must recognize that the first Christians did not understand from the very beginning all the implications of what they believed and did, and the different books of the New Testament often show different stages of understanding.

Chapter 1: The Church Begins in Jerusalem

dence in early Christian missionary endeavor of people being free to say, "I now believe in Jesus," and then walking off on their own—they are made part of a community. This is important theologically. Peter is telling people that they can be saved, but not simply as individuals. The basic Israelite concept is that God chose to save *a people*, and the renewal of the covenant on Pentecost has not changed that. There is a collective aspect to salvation, and one is saved as part of God's people. The importance of the church is a direct derivative from the importance of Israel.

Once again Acts is almost prescient in anticipating what should be part of our understanding of Christian essentials today. We all know that there is a division among Christian churches. Yet there may be a more dangerous division among Christians. I have often thought that in the 21st century the deepest chasm experienced in Christianity may be between those who, although they worship in various churches, think "church" is important, and those for whom Christianity is really a matter of "Jesus and me," without any concept of being saved as part of a people or church.

Third, Peter specifies that baptism must be "in the name of Jesus Christ." The fact that John the Baptist baptized and that Jesus himself was baptized by John was surely an important factor in moving the followers of Jesus to insist on baptism; yet Acts 18:24–19:7 contends that there was a clear distinction between the baptism of John and baptism "in the name of the Lord Jesus" (19:5). We are not certain about procedures in the earliest Christian baptism; but most likely "in the name of" means that the one being baptized confessed who Jesus was (and in that sense spoke his name),[14]

---

[14] This early, of course, we are not reading about infant baptism; and so it is less likely that the person conducting the baptism had to say the formula over the persons being baptized: They could speak for themselves. As I explained in *A Risen Christ at Eastertime*, the use of the triadic formula in Matt 28:19 would have been a later development giving a fuller picture of God's plan of salvation.

The Response

e.g., "Jesus is Lord"; "Jesus is the Messiah (Christ)"; "Jesus is the Son of God"; "Jesus is the Son of Man."[15] Such baptismal confessions would explain why titles were so commonly applied to Jesus in the New Testament. From the very beginning the identity of Jesus' followers was established by what they believed and professed about Jesus. (Our later creeds are an enlarged expression of the faith expressed at baptism.) This was a startling difference from Judaism; for although one could call Jews "disciples of Moses" (John 9:28), no one would ever think of defining them by what they believed about the personal identity of Moses. The need to give expression to the centrality of Jesus in the new covenant made Christianity a creedal religion in a manner dissimilar to Judaism.

•Here again I see Acts giving us valuable guidance about Christian fundamentals. I have often thought it would be a fascinating exercise some Sunday to ask everyone in church to write on a slip of paper one sentence explaining what a Christian is. My suspicion is that many of the responses would consist of behavioral descriptions, e.g., a Christian is one who practices love of neighbor. True, one cannot be much of a Christian without behaving as Jesus taught, but behavior is not sufficiently defining: Christians are not the only ones who exhibit love toward each other. It would be fascinating to know how many would answer that a Christian is one who believes that Jesus is the Christ. That, of course, is both the most ancient and basic definition. We may well need to reiterate today what seemed so obvious to our original ancestors in the faith.

Fourth, after spelling out the demands on those who believe in Jesus, in 2:38-39 Peter makes a promise: "You shall

[15] John 9:35-38 may be echoing a baptismal ceremony in that church: a question from the baptizer, "Do you believe in the Son of Man?"; a responding question from the one to be baptized, "Who is he that I may believe?"; a response from the baptizer "Jesus"; a response from the one who is to be baptized, "Lord, I believe"; and then an act of worship.

Chapter 1: The Church Begins in Jerusalem

receive the gift of the Holy Spirit, for the promise is . . . to as many as the Lord God calls." (The last clause reminds us that although there is a challenge to the hearers to change their lives, the priority in conversion belongs to God.[16]) Peter and his companions have received the Holy Spirit, and now they promise that the same Holy Spirit will be given to all believers. In terms of the fundamentals of Christian life there will be no second-class citizens, and the same equality in receiving the gift of the Spirit will prove true when the first Gentiles are baptized (Acts 10:44-48). That there was no privileged class in what really mattered was an enormously attractive factor in evangelizing, and even in today's church it is worth emphasizing. Inevitably when the church received more structure, different roles were assigned to individuals; and some were ordained, i.e., put in a certain order. Such specialization, necessary as it was, has produced envy and bickering in the church. We can see that already in I Corinthians 12. Some are apostles, some are prophets, some are teachers, etc.; and in order to overcome the fact that those who have one gift envy those who have another, Paul has to stress that these are all gifts of one and the same Spirit, meant to build up the one body into which all are baptized. The same holds true today when we bicker over who can hold which roles in the church. These roles may be visibly important in terms of public prestige and even power. But we need to be reminded that they all pale when compared to the basic gift given to all: baptism and the Holy Spirit. When we stand before the throne of God and church offices are no more, our dignity will depend on the extent to which we have remained faithful to our common baptismal calling and have lived by the one Spirit given to all.

[16] Acts 2:40 is sometimes translated, "Save yourselves from this crooked generation"; but from a theological viewpoint the passive is better rendered literally: "Be saved." People cannot save themsevles; they can respond to God's saving grace.

The Response

Chapter 2

The Jerusalem Church of One Mind
(Acts 2:42-5:42)

Acts has told us that many of those who heard Peter's sermons met his demands and were baptized (about three thousand people!). Now the author turns to describe how they lived. The memories he reports are highly selective, so that we have as much a theology of the early church as a history. First, he summarizes under four headings the relations of Christians[17] with one another (2:42-47) and then, in a continuous narrative highlighting Peter and John, their relations to others (3:1–5:42). Historically the setting would be the first years in Jerusalem, from Jesus' death and resurrection (AD 30 or 33) until about 36—a period that, surely with idealization, he describes as the time when the believers were of one mind (1:14; 2:46; 4:24; 5:12). Liturgically, six readings from this section of Acts are found in the different cycles of the 2d, 3d, and 4th Sundays of Easter, and nine consecutive readings constitute pericopes on weekdays of the 1st and 2d Week of Easter.

FOUR CHARACTERISTICS SUMMARIZING RELATIONS AMONG BELIEVERS (ACTS 2:42-47)

One of the notable marks of Acts, especially in the first part, is to give brief summaries of the early Christian situation, generalizing what is happening. The present section consti-

[17] I am aware that throughout these early chapters of Acts, which treat of immediately postresurrectional Jerusalem, to speak of Christians or Christianity is an anachronism; no designation had as yet been found for those who believed in Jesus. If the author of Acts is historically correct, it was at Antioch (seemingly in the late 30s) that the believers were first called Christians. Yet having noted that, for the sake of simplicity I shall anticipate the terminology.

tutes an admirable summary of how ideally the first believers in Jesus related to one another. Singled out are four features[18] that I shall treat in this order: koinōnia, prayers, breaking of the bread, and apostles' teaching.

Koinōnia (Fellowship, Communion). In chapter 1 above, I pointed out that, although in his public ministry Jesus showed little interest in a formally distinct society, his followers by introducing baptism showed a remarkable drive toward having believers "join up." Those who believed belonged to a group. The wide distribution in the New Testament of the term *koinōnia* (related to *koinos*, "common" as in Koinē Greek), shows that those who were baptized felt strongly that they had much in common. Sometimes it is translated as "fellowship," although that is a rather weak term. More literally it is "communion," i.e., the spirit that binds people together, or "community," i.e., the grouping produced by that spirit. Indeed, *koinōnia* may reflect in Greek an early Semitic name for the Jewish group of believers in Jesus, comparable to the self-designation of the Jewish Dead Sea Scrolls group as the *Yaḥad*, "the oneness, unity."[19]

---

[18] The selection is made from the later vantage point of the author: features that have been the most important and enduring. There is an idealization, not in the crude sense of creating a fictional picture, but in holding up the primitive community as embodying what a Christian community should be. In the first five chapters of Acts equal time is not given to the problems and faults of the Jerusalem community.

[19] Another early name may have been "the Way," e.g., Acts 24:14: "According to the Way . . . I worship the God of our Fathers" (also Acts 9:2; 19:9, 23; 22:4; 24:22). This was also a Dead Sea Scrolls self-designation: "When these people join the community (*Yaḥad*), they . . . go into the wilderness to prepare the way of the Lord." This reflects the idealism of the return of Israel from exile (Isaiah 40:3), when Israel came along the way prepared by God to the Promised Land. The designation that became the most popular, i.e., *ekklēsia*, "church," plausibly reflects the first exodus in which Israel came into being, for in Deuteronomy 23:2 the Greek Old Testament rendered *qāhāl*, "assembly," by *ekklēsia* to describe Israel in the desert as "the church of the Lord."

Relations Among Believers

An important aspect of the *koinōnia* described in Acts 2:44-47; 5:1-11 is voluntary sharing of goods among the members of the community. While the idealism of Acts probably exaggerates in referring to "all goods," the fact that there were common goods among the Dead Sea Scrolls group shows that a picture of sharing is plausible for a Jewish group convinced that the last times had begun and that this world's wealth has lost its meaning.[20] Sharing goods and livelihood bind people together closely—a person really makes a commitment when he or she puts funds into a common bank account with someone else. Part of the goal of the Jerusalem community's sharing was that there might be no members who were totally impoverished. The actual result, however, may have been that most of the community were relatively poor. Paul refers several times to the poor (Christians) in Jerusalem for whom he was collecting money (Romans 15:26; Galatians 2:10; I Corinthians 16:1-3). The willingness of Gentiles in distant churches to share some of their wealth with the Jewish Christians in Jerusalem was for Paul a tangible proof of the *koinōnia* that bound Christians together.

Of course, *koinōnia* was a wider concept than the sharing of goods; it involved common faith and common salvation. How intrinsic it was to Christianity is exemplified in Galatians 2:9 where Paul deems the outcome of the discussion in Jerusalem *ca.* AD 49 about the fate of the Gentile churches to have been a great success because at the end the leaders of the Jerusalem church gave to him and Barnabas the right hand of *koinōnia*. For Paul it would have been against the

---

[20] More than other Gospels Luke is insistent that wealth is an obstacle to the acceptance of Jesus' standards and that the rich are endangered (1:53; 6:24; 12:20-21; 16:22-23). Sometimes it is contended that Luke has deeschatologized Christianity in the sense that he has recognized that Christians do not know the times or seasons for the final intervention of God's rule/kingdom (Acts 1:7). That does not mean that he has given up his hope for the second coming or lost his estimation of values consonant with a theology in which this world is not a lasting entity.

Chapter 2: The Jerusalem Church of One Mind

very notion of the one Lord and the one Spirit if the *koinōnia* between the Jewish and the Gentile churches had been broken. Only toward the end of the New Testament period do we get clear evidence that the Christian *koinōnia* has been broken. The author of I John sees the necessity of having *koinōnia* "with us" in order to have *koinōnia* with the Father and the Holy Spirit, and he considers "those who went out from us" to be the antichrists (1:3; 2:18-19).

As with other aspects of Acts' portrayal of the early church, the notion of *koinōnia* needs emphasis in our time. There is, first of all, the great scandal of Christians living in churches that have broken *koinōnia* with each other; and the whole purpose of ecumenism is to see if we can regain that communion. And a more immediate scandal is our sudden tendency within Roman Catholicism to break the *koinōnia*. For centuries after the 16th-century Reformation we took pride (somewhat gloatingly) in the fact that Catholics were united while the Protestant churches seem to splinter over and over again. Yet now after the 20th-century self-reformation at Vatican II, we are splintering. On the ultraconservative extreme there is the movement of Archbishop Lefebvre which is convinced that it is remaining faithful to the church by breaking from the Bishop of Rome. On the liberal extreme there are small conventicles attempting to celebrate the eucharist without ordained clergy, thinking they are reduplicating the life of the early communities. Often this is justified by the claim "We are the church" (probably with the supposition that the clergy or hierarchy are claiming to be the church). Should not all Catholic Christians recognize that they can claim no more than that they are *part* of the church—part of a much larger *koinōnia* that includes the presiding presence of the bishop[21] (and for the whole church, the presiding presence of

[21] At the beginning of the 2d century Ignatius of Antioch is an eloquent exponent of this: "Make sure that no step affecting the church is ever taken without the bishop" (*Smyrnaeans* 8:1); "I must count you blessed who are united with your bishop, just as the church is united with Jesus Christ"

Relations Among Believers

the Bishop of Rome)? Breaking from that *koinōnia* is scarcely reduplicating the values of the early church.

Prayers. Praying for each other was another aspect of *koinōnia*, and the Pauline letters bear eloquent testimony to his constant prayer for the communities he founded. Here, since we are considering the description of the first Christians in Acts, it might be fruitful to reflect on what kind of prayer forms were used by those Jews who came to believe in Jesus. Of course, since they did not cease to be Jewish in their worship, they continued to say prayers that they had known previously. When Mark wrote, the primacy of the basic Jewish confession, the *Shema* ("Hear O Israel, the Lord our God, the Lord is one"), was still being inculcated even for Gentiles (12:29). I share the view of many scholars that the hymns of the Lucan infancy narrative, the *Magnificat*, the *Benedictus*, the *Gloria*, and the *Nunc Dimittis*, were early Christian compositions that Luke took over and adapted in placing them on the lips of the first characters of his Gospel. Like the Jewish hymns of this time (as exemplified in the Books of the Maccabees and the Dead Sea Scrolls) they are a pastiche of Old Testament echoes. They celebrate what God has done in Jesus; yet they are not christological in the sense of giving details from the life of Jesus. (Contrast the hymns of Philippians 2:6-11; Colossians 1:15-20; John 1:1-18.) The Benedictus is a marvelous example: Something tremendous has happened; but it is described in terms of Abraham, David, the biblical ancestors, and the prophets.[22]

In addition to these common Jewish prayer patterns the early Christians adopted Jesus' own prayer style, still visible in the Lord's Prayer which is preserved in different forms in Matthew 6:9-13 and Luke 11:2-4; but, of course, some petitions of the Lord's Prayer echo petitions of synagogue

---

(*Ephesians* 5:1); "You must never act independently of your bishop and presbyters" (*Magnesians* 7:1).

[22] In my judgment 1:76-77 represents Luke's adaptation to the context.

Chapter 2: The Jerusalem Church of One Mind

prayers. It is important to notice the eschatological tone of that prayer which asks the heavenly Father to cause the divine name to be praised (hallowed), to bring about the kingdom, and to make the divine will all-effective on earth—in other words, which asks God to bring in the endtime. Then the prayer turns to the share of the Christians in the endtime: to be forgiven in the judgment, not to be led into the fearsome trial, and to escape the power of the Evil One.[23] This eschatological tone of Christian prayer is intimately linked to a fervent expectation that Christ would come again soon. A very ancient Christian prayer transcribed from Aramaic, *Maranatha*, "Our Lord, come," has the same tone and is more specifically christological. And indeed inevitably Christian prayer did center on recalling and praising what Jesus had done, a development one is tempted to associate with the increasing Christian awareness of distinctiveness from other Jews.

Breaking Bread. Acts portrays early Christians like Peter and John going frequently, or even daily, to the Temple to pray at the regular hours (2:46; 3:1; 5:12, 21, 42). This implies that the first Jews who believed in Jesus saw no rupture in their ordinary worship pattern. The "breaking of bread" (presumably the eucharist) would, then, have been in addition to and not in place of the sacrifices and worship of Israel. Notice the sequence in 2:46: "Day by day attending the Temple together and breaking bread in their homes." How did the first Christians interpret the eucharist? Paul, writing in the mid-50s (I Corinthians 11:23-26), mentions a eucharistic pattern that was handed on to him (presumably, therefore, from the 30s) and says, "As often as you eat this

[23] See "The Pater Noster as an Eschatological Prayer" in my *New Testament Essays* (New York: Paulist, 1982 reprint), 217-53, for the idea that *peirasmos* originally referred to the trial of the endtime (not simply to daily temptation), and for fact that *epiousios*, the word that most often has been translated as "daily," may not mean that.

Relations Among Believers

bread and drink this cup, you proclaim the Lord's death until he comes." The recalling of the Lord's death *may* echo the Jewish pattern of Passover re-presentation (Hebrew: *zikkārôn*; Greek: *anamnēsis*), making present again the great salvific act, now shifted from the exodus to the crucifixion/resurrection. The "until he comes" reflects the eschatological outlook we saw above in the Lord's Prayer and *Maranatha*. Attached, however, to a sacred meal it may have a special Jewish background. In the Dead Sea Scrolls community there was left vacant at the sacred repast a place for the Messiah in case God should raise him up during the meal. The thought that Jesus would come back at the celebration of the eucharist may be related to the tradition that the risen Jesus showed himself present at meals (Luke 24:30, 41; John 21:9-13; Mark 16:14), so that his disciples recognized him in the breaking of the bread (Luke 24:35). As we reflect on these different details, we can find the background of much of the later theology of the eucharist, e.g., the celebration of the eucharist as a sacrifice can be related to recalling the death of the Lord, and the concept of the real presence of Christ in the eucharist can be related to believing that the risen Lord appeared at meals and would return again at the sacred meal.

A Jewish pattern may also have affected the Christian choice of a time for eating the eucharistic meal. Undoubtedly, the discovery of the empty tomb early Sunday morning helped to fix Christian attention on what by the end of the 1st century would be known as "the Lord's Day." Yet the choice of Sunday may have also been facilitated by the pattern of the Jewish Sabbath which ended at sundown on Saturday. Before sundown Jews who believed in Jesus did not have extensive freedom of movement; but when the Sabbath was over (Saturday evening), they would have been free to come from a distance to assemble in the house of another believer to break the bread. This may explain why the ancient Christian memory is of a celebration on the night between Saturday and Sunday. Such a eucharistic assembly

Chapter 2: The Jerusalem Church of One Mind

would be a major manifestation of *koinōnia* and eventually help to make Christians feel distinct from other Jews.

Teaching of the Apostles. Authoritative for all Jews were the Scriptures, in particular the Law and the Prophets; this would have been true for the first followers of Jesus as well. Thus, early Christian teaching would for the most part have been Jewish teaching.[24] Points where Jesus modified or differed from the Law or from the Pharisee interpretation of the Law were remembered and became the nucleus of a special teaching. As they passed this on, the Christian preachers would have made their own application to situations that Jesus had not encountered; and the content stemming from Jesus in the teaching would have been expanded by apostolic teaching. (See the example of two instructions on marriage and divorce, one from the Lord and one from Paul, in I Corinthians 7:10, 12.) This teaching of Jesus and of the apostles, while secondary to the teaching of the Jewish Scriptures, was more authoritative in regard to the specific points it touched. When such teaching was committed to writing, these writings had within themselves the possibility of becoming a second set of Scriptures (the New Testament).[25] An understanding of the dynamics of distinctive Christian thought is very useful today as we seek to emphasize that

[24] This fact is sometimes overlooked by those who search out New Testament theology or ethics. The points of unique importance mentioned in the New Testament are like the tip of the iceberg, the bulk of which is the unmentioned, presupposed teaching of Israel.

[25] The gathering of writings was a part of the canon-forming process particularly active in the late 2d century. During the same period a somewhat similar process within rabbinic Judaism produced the Mishna, a second set of teachings alongside the Scriptures. Thus by the end of the 2d century both those who believed in Jesus and the Jews who did not had written authoritative supplements to the Law and the Prophets. The different character of the two writings (one a collection of stories about Jesus and the early church, letters to the churches, and an apocalypse; the other a collection of legal interpretations) reflects essential differences in the respective religious focuses.

Relations Among Believers

the Old Testament (i.e., the Law and the Prophets) is not simply an interesting prelude to the really important New Testament, but the basic presupposition of the New Testament with which we must be familiar to be fully Christian.

In reflecting on the four characteristics of relations among Christians that Acts mentions, I have emphasized two aspects of the picture: continuity with Judaism, and the distinctive features that marked off the community of Jews who believed in Jesus from the rest of Jews. These aspects were in tension, pulling in opposite directions: The first held the Christians close to their fellow Jews who met in the synagogues; the second gave to the Christian *koinōnia* identity and the potentiality of self-sufficiency. External factors of rejection and reaction, however, would have to take place before Christians would constitute a distinguishably separate religious group, and that development will be the subject of later chapters of Acts. Before that we should consider three chapters in which Acts describes the earliest interactions of those who now believed in Jesus with their fellow Jews.

NARRATIVES HIGHLIGHTING THE RELATIONS OF
EARLY CHRISTIANS TO OTHERS (ACTS 3:1-5:42)
In these chapters Acts will use the actions of Peter and John to focus narratives that involve the first Jewish believers in Jesus with their Jerusalem neighbors who do not share that belief, a relationship that will produce more conversions and much opposition.

Acts 3:1-26: A Healing and the Preaching that Follows. In 2:43 Acts mentioned in passing that many wonders and signs were done through the apostles; in 2:46 it was said that day by day they attended the Temple together. Those summary statements were meant to prepare the way for the account in 3:1-10 of the healing that takes place when Peter and John go up to the Temple. The story is told with a real sense of drama. The lapidary statement of Peter catches the spirit of

Chapter 2: The Jerusalem Church of One Mind

the Christian self-understanding that what we have to offer is different from what the world, even at its best, can give: "Silver and gold I have none, but what I have, I give you: In the name of Jesus Christ of Nazareth walk." Luke's Gospel showed Jesus beginning his ministry by manifesting the healing power of God's rule (kingdom) to the amazement of all (4:31-37); Acts has the clear intention of showing that Peter and the apostles carried on the same work with the same power. The healing is "in the name of Jesus Christ of Nazareth," i.e., worked through the power of the heavenly Christ, not through any self-sufficiency of the apostles. And yet there is more in this reference to "the name" than we may first notice. We have heard that believers had to be baptized "in the name of Jesus." To know a person's name is to know his identity; to know that Jesus is the Messiah, the Lord, the Son of God is to know his christological identity. There is power in the knowledge of that name (christological identity), and faith in it opens access to that power: "By faith in his name, his name has made this [lame] man strong" (Acts 3:16). Respect for the personal name of God (YHWH or Yahweh) and the awesome power it possessed caused Jews not to mention it publicly. (In Jewish legend when the Pharaoh kept questioning Moses as to who was this God who demanded that the people be let go, the exasperated Moses finally used the name of God; and the Pharaoh was struck to the ground.[26]) Christians developed a similar awe for the name given to Jesus, as we see in Philippians 2:9-11: "Therefore God has highly exalted him and graciously bestowed on him the name that is above every other name, so that at the name possessed by Jesus every knee should bow in heaven, on earth, and under the earth, and every tongue confess that Jesus Christ is Lord."

[26] In antiChristian Jewish polemical stories in circulation by the end of the 2d century, the (evil) power of Jesus was attributed to the fact that he had gone to Egypt, learned magic, and had the divine name sewn into his thigh.

Relations of Early Christians to Others

The Lucan account of Jesus' ministry combined his healings and his words; here in a similar pattern Peter's healing is followed by a sermon (Acts 3:11-26). The author idealizes the situation by speaking of those who see and hear as "all the people" (3:9) or "the people" (3:12). This sermon is presented as an embodiment of how preachers presented Jesus to Jews. As with Peter's sermon on Pentecost, it amalgamates Old Testament echoes and what God has done in Jesus. If the Pentecost sermon began its challenge with the prophecy of Joel that was seen to be fulfilled in what was happening, this sermon will terminate (3:22-26) with a challenge based on the promise of Moses in Deuteronomy 18:15-19 that God would raise up a prophet like him who must be listened to. In 3:19 the demand to "repent" or "change one's mind" (*metanoein*) appears once more, but now there is greater specification. The Jews of Jerusalem delivered up and denied Jesus the servant of God in the presence of Pilate who had decided to release him (3:13); they denied the Holy and Just One and asked for a murderer (3:14: Barabbas). Yet they acted in ignorance as did their rulers,[27] and accordingly they are being offered this chance to change. Ours is a time when because of past tragedies we are trying to learn not to generalize responsibility for evil actions, and so it is painful to see in the New Testament the generalizing of Jewish responsibility for the execution of Jesus (here literally: "men [*andres*] of Israel"; Matt 27:25: "all the people"; I Thessalonians 2:14-15: "the Jews who killed both the Lord Jesus and the prophets"). Luke-Acts, at least, shows some sensibilities on the subject

[27] The language of Acts echoes the Lucan account of the passion: There Pilate could find no guilt in Jesus and wanted to release him (Luke 23:4, 14-15, 20-22); Barabbas was said to have committed murder (23:19, 25); the centurion confessed Jesus to be just (23:47); and Jesus prayed for those who crucify him, "Father, forgive them; for they know not what they do" (23:34a). In my *The Death of the Messiah* (2 vols.; New York: Doubleday, 1994), 2.§40, I argue that 23:34a, although missing from many mss. of Luke, is more likely genuine.

Chapter 2: The Jerusalem Church of One Mind

by showing that not all the people were against Jesus (Luke 23:27, 48) and that those who were did not consciously choose to do something evil (also Acts 13:27).[28] In face of the apostolic preaching, however, ignorance is no longer an excuse, and change of mind/heart is necessary if they are to receive Jesus as the Messiah when he is sent back from heaven (Acts 3:19-21). The story that follows will maintain that many of the people did change, but most of the Jewish leaders did not. In the late 50s Paul confidently foresaw that the salvation that had come to the Gentiles would make those who went by the name Israel jealous and ultimately lead to their full inclusion (Romans 11:11-12). By the time Acts was written (80s or 90s of the 1st century?), the situation had hardened. Acts will end its story in Rome with the very harsh judgment that, as Isaiah foretold, this people will never hear or understand, and therefore the salvation wrought by God in Christ has been sent to the Gentiles who will listen (28:25-29). Of course, the author of Acts did not mean that from this moment on Christians would no longer receive into the church Jews who came to believe in Christ, but he no longer expected the mission to the Jews to bear much fruit.

Acts 4:1-31: The Antagonism of the Sanhedrin and the Apostolic Refusal to Yield. The apostolic preaching and its success (4:4: five thousand) is portrayed as stirring up the wrath of the priests and the Sadducees who arrest Peter and John. Jesus' own attitude toward resurrection had aroused the opposition of the Sadducees "who say there is no resurrection" (Luke 20:27-38), and so Acts is once more creating a parallelism between Jesus and the apostles in having the Sadducees disturbed that Peter and John have been proclaiming in Jesus the resurrection from the dead (Acts 4:2). A meeting of the Sanhedrin consisting of rulers, elders, scribes, and chief priests is convened against them (4:5-6), just as a Sanhedrin

[28] Notice also the thesis in Romans 10:3 that it was out of ignorance that Israel according to the flesh did not submit to God's righteousness in Christ.

Relations of Early Christians to Others

of the elders of the people, and chief priests and scribes was convened against Jesus (Luke 22:66). (In neither case are the Pharisees mentioned as having directly involved, and that may be historical.) They focus on the miracle, demanding, "By what name did you this?"—a question that prepares for the response of Peter emphasizing anew what we have already heard: "by the name of Jesus Christ of Nazareth whom you crucified, whom God raised from the dead. . . . There is no other name under heaven given to the human race by which we must be saved" (Acts 4:10, 12).

Luke did not report in his Gospel the annoyed wonderment of the people of Nazareth that Jesus, who was only a carpenter, could teach wisely (Mark 6:1-3). That omission may have been prompted by Luke's attested reluctance to report what was derogatory of Jesus. By way of compensation Acts 4:13 reports the annoyed wonderment of the authorities at the boldness of the religious proclamation of the apostles who were not formally educated in religious matters or the Law of Moses.[29] Trapped by the clear factuality of the healing that had been performed, the Sanhedrin authorities blusteringly cut short any debate by arbitrarily ordering Peter and John not to speak in the name of Jesus (4:18). This prepares for an unforgettably defiant response of Peter (4:19-20). Less than two months before, Peter in the high priest's house had denied Jesus three times; now before a battery of chief priests he cannot be silent about Christ. Among the Gospels Luke alone (22:31-32) had Jesus pray that, although Satan desired to sift Peter and the others like wheat, his faith would not fail and he would turn and strengthen his brethren. Here we see the prayer fulfilled as Peter and John emerge unyielding from the Sanhedrin to report to their fellow believers what has happened—a report that consists of a triumphal prayer of praise to God (Acts 4:24-30) comparing

[29] Through the centuries many have used the reference in Acts 4:13 to the apostles as being untrained in letters to portray them as illiterate. That is unnecessary.

Chapter 2: The Jerusalem Church of One Mind

the forces that had been aligned in Jerusalem against Jesus (Herod and Pilate, the Gentiles and the "peoples" of Israel) to the forces now uttering threats against his followers. In a literary flourish this prayer is described as shaking the place where they are. They are all filled with the Holy Spirit and, thus strengthened, proceed to speak the word of God with boldness (4:31). Matthew (27:51; 28:2) had the earth quake as a manifestation of supportive divine power when Jesus died and rose; Acts has it quake as the Holy Spirit manifests God's supporting presence in the community of believers. Peter's catalyzing role in this fulfills Jesus' promise to him in Luke 22:32.

Acts 4:32–5:11: Another Description of the Relations among Believers. After Peter's initial sermon on Pentecost to the Jerusalem populace, Acts (2:41-47) stopped to summarize how those who listened and believed related to one another as a community. Now again (4:32-35), as a demonstration that they were of one heart and soul, we are given a summary description emphasizing some of the same features, especially that they held things in common (*koinos*). This time, however, the summary is followed by two examples. The first involves Joseph, surnamed by the apostles Barnabas, who sold a field and brought the money to the apostles to contribute to the common fund. Besides exemplifying positively the spirit of *koinōnia,* this reference prepares for future narrative. Barnabas is a levite, and Acts 6:7 will tell us that many priests came to believe; thus the faith would make its way even among those most opposed to Jesus. Moreover, Barnabas is from Cyprus; and when later at Antioch he becomes a missionary with Paul, they will first go to Cyprus (13:1-4).

The other example, involving Ananias and Sapphira (5:1-11), is negative and illustrates divine punishment of those who violated the purity of the early community. It does not constitute a reading in the Easter season, perhaps a tacit recognition that God's striking people dead is too chilling for

Relations of Early Christians to Others

modern religious sensibilities. Yet no story illustrates better the Israelite mentality of the early believers. The Twelve were meant to sit on thrones judging the tribes of Israel (Luke 22:30); here judgment is exercised on the renewed Israel through Peter. In the Old Testament (Joshua 7) Israel's attempt to enter victoriously beyond Jericho into the heart of the Promised Land was frustrated because Achan had secretly hidden for himself goods that were to be dedicated to God. His deception caused God to judge that Israel had sinned and needed purification, for the people had to be perfect. Only when Achan was put to death and his goods burned could Israel proceed as the people of God. So also the renewed Israel has been profaned by the deceptive holding back of goods which were claimed to have been contributed to the common fund. Satan entered into Judas, one of the Twelve, to give Jesus over (Luke 22:3-4); and now he has entered into the heart of Ananias, a believer in Jesus, to be deceptive in relation to the Holy Spirit that has brought this community of believers into being (Acts 5:3). Such impurity must be eradicated, and that can be accomplished only by the judgment of Peter which brings about the fatal action of God. (We are very close here to an early understanding of the power to bind and to loose!) It is in describing the fear produced by this intervention that Acts uses the term "church" for the first time (5:11). Obviously the author does not think that such an act of judgment is alien to the nature of the church. We might wonder how he would react to the church's omission of the reading in an Eastertime Lectionary that contains all the surrounding passages.

Acts 5:12-42: The Second Confrontation with the Sanhedrin. The author of Luke-Acts likes to pair passages symmetrically in order to convey the intensification of an issue, and that is true in this second confrontation of the apostles with the Sanhedrin. No longer one healing, but many signs and wonders are involved. People even from the surrounding vil-

Chapter 2: The Jerusalem Church of One Mind

lages begin to bring their sick to be cured by the apostles, especially by Peter. Once again the high priests and the Sadducees have the apostles arrested but are frustrated when an angel of the Lord releases them so that they return to the Temple—a release all the more ironical because the Sadducees do not believe in angels. Thus the Sanhedrin session called to discuss the apostles has to have them arrested again. As with the arrest of Jesus (Luke 22:6) care has to be taken not to arouse the people (Acts 5:26). When the high priest indignantly recalls that the apostles had been charged not to teach in Jesus' name, again Peter expresses his defiance with a memorable line: "We must obey God rather than human beings" and then gives a christological sermon as though he hoped to convert the Sanhedrin (Acts 5:30-32).

The infuriation reaches the point of wanting to kill the apostles (5:33), when the Pharisee Gamaliel I intervenes. Scholars have debated endlessly whether this part of the scene is historical.[30] At least it does not lack chronological verisimilitude, for the great Gamaliel lived in Jerusalem at this time. Far more important, however, is the place of the scene in the Lucan storyline. Acts has not mentioned Pharisees as opposed to the followers of Jesus; and now it has Gamaliel the Pharisee advocating tolerance for them. Later (23:6-9) Acts will have the Pharisees supporting tolerance for Paul over against the Sadducees. Reference to Gamaliel is harmonious in another way, for Acts (22:3) will present Paul as having studied with this great teacher of the Law who here is depicted as a fair-minded man. Offering examples of other movements that failed, Gamaliel summarizes the situation, "If this work be from human beings, it will fail; if it is from God, you will not be able to overthrow it."[31]

[30] There are anachronisms in Gamaliel's speech, e.g., he mentions Theudas' revolt and "after him Judas the Galilean." If this Sanhedrin session took place around AD 36, Theudas' revolt had not yet taken place, and Judas' revolt had taken place thirty years before.

[31] Acts 23:6-9 will show Pharisees siding with the Christian position on

Relations of Early Christians to Others

(It may not be true that every religious movement that is of human origin fails; nevertheless, the church would have been wiser many times in its history if it had used Gamaliel's principle to judge new developments in Christianity rather than reacting in a hostile manner too quickly.) Gamaliel's advice carries the day. Although the apostles are beaten, they are let go; and tacitly the Sanhedrin adopts the policy of leaving them alone as they continue every day to preach Christ publicly and privately (5:42).

Brief Reflections on John 3 and John 6

As explained in the *Introduction*, I do not plan to comment on the passages from John in themselves, but only as they are related to the Acts readings in the Easter season. Acts describes the external or visible history of early Christian life. Working through Jesus' words, John gives a theological insight into the internal relations of Christians to Jesus. In the liturgical weeks when the Acts readings discussed in chapters 1 and 2 are being read on weekdays, the Gospel selections are from John 3 and John 6.[32] In Acts we heard Peter's challenge to those who would be the first Christians, a challenge to be baptized and receive the Holy Spirit. In the description of their lives as a community we heard of the breaking of the bread as part of the *koinōnia* that held them together. It is no accident that the accompanying readings from John 3 deal with being born again of water and Spirit, and those from John 6 deal with eating the bread of life. Acts plays out its story against the background of opposition from the chief priests and the members of the Sanhedrin. John 3 consists largely of a dialogue with Nicodemus, a member of the

---

resurrection against the Sadducees, but that is not offered by Gamaliel in the present situation as the reason for toleration.

[32] The selections from John 6 overlap into the 3d Week of Easter.

Chapter 2: The Jerusalem Church of One Mind

Sanhedrin who does not understand Jesus; John 6, set in a synagogue, involves a debate over Scripture with Jews who think Jesus' claims are impossible.

John 3. This first great dialogue/discourse in John deals with the most basic gift that the Son of Man has brought from heaven to earth, eternal life.[33] The opening verses are the only reference in John to "the kingdom of God," which is a central theme of Jesus throughout the Synoptic Gospels. John immediately translates that motif into the language of eternal life which is a central theme in the Fourth Gospel. This simple and yet profound image is based on the all-important fact that Jesus is God's only, unique Son, a dignity never possessed by anyone before or after. In particular Jesus is compared to Moses who, after going up the mountain to speak with God, came down to reveal God's will. Jesus as God's Son was already with God and had only to come down to reveal. A human parent possesses earthly life (a life that ends in death); God has eternal life. Human beings receive earthly life from their parents; Jesus, as God's Son, has eternal life from the heavenly Father. As the Word become flesh, he and he alone can give this eternal life to those whose human life he shares. Those who believe in him receive it.

To Nicodemus who approaches him as a teacher from God[34] Jesus explains how this takes place. For eternal life

---

[33] To understand the uniqueness of John among the Gospels it is necessary to recognize that the others never refer to a previous life that the Son shared with the Father; they are never specific about an incarnation. Whereas for them Jesus is the Son of Man during his earthly ministry and will come back from heaven as the Son of Man at the end of time, for John Jesus on earth has already come from heaven as the Son of Man. Please note: I am not saying that the first three evangelists deny or would deny an incarnation, but simply that there is nothing in their writings that shows they were aware of it. An awareness is found, however, in other non-Gospel passages in the New Testament (Philippians [probably]; Colossians; Hebrews).

[34] He thinks Jesus has been raised up by God whereas Jesus has actually

Brief Reflections on John 3 and John 6

even as for earthly life begetting or birth is necessary, yet from God above, not from earthly parents. This is a radical challenge to the Judaism of which Nicodemus is a leading representative, a Judaism for which membership in the chosen people of God comes from birth from a Jewish mother. To that Jesus responds that flesh begets only flesh, so that the identity or status of one's earthly parents makes no difference whatsoever so far as relationship to God is concerned—it takes the Spirit to beget spirit. And so begetting/birth from God above is a begetting/birth of water and Spirit.

In discussing baptism in Acts, I commented that there are many different New Testament theologies of baptism. John sees it as a birth through which the Spirit gives God's very life; consequently those believers begotten/born of water and Spirit are God's own children. In the Synoptic Gospels we hear that one has to become like a little child to inherit the kingdom; John has radicalized that idea to an insistence on being born from God as a child.

Nicodemus, of course, does not understand how this can be (3:9) because he thinks on an earthly level and does not recognize that it is one from heaven who speaks to him. In the dialogue that follows (which now becomes a monologue) Jesus explains in various ways the great sweep of descent from heaven and return to heaven (through being lifted up on the cross) involved in the incarnation. Others may emphasize judgment at the end of time; but for John, since God manifested love by giving the only Son to come among us, that coming constitutes judgment. People must decide either for the light that has come into the world or for darkness.

The sudden switch to a setting involving John the Baptist

---

come from God. A commentary on the Gospel will explain the many plays on Greek words in this passage, e.g., the same word means "begetting by" (a father) and "born from" (a mother); the same word means "again" and "from above"; the same word means "wind" and "spirit."

Chapter 2: The Jerusalem Church of One Mind

(3:22ff.) helps to specify that what Jesus has been speaking about does involve baptism, hitherto not mentioned by name. Indeed we are told that Jesus himself baptized. As mentioned in chapter 1 above, in the Synoptic Gospels we are never told that Jesus baptized anyone; and his command to others to baptize (Matt 28:19) comes only after the resurrection. Consequently one could get the impression that baptism, which is an extremely important part of church life, was quite foreign to Jesus' own life and practice. The Fourth Gospel brings baptism as a begetting/birth of water and Spirit very much into the context of Jesus' life since it is one of the first issues he introduces when he discusses the purpose of his coming. Thus no longer can there be a dichotomy between what Jesus said and did and what the church says and does; one continues the other.

John 6. The same may be said about the eucharist. The three Synoptic Gospels localize the eucharistic action of Jesus at the Last Supper before he dies and have a specific reference to the shedding of his blood which will take place the next day. Paul sees the eucharist as recalling the death of the Lord until he comes. That magnificent conception leaves difficulties. Is the eucharist so attached to Jesus' death that it is unrelated to what he did earlier during his public ministry, and once again do we have a dichotomy between what he normally did and what is central in church life? How often should one recall or make present the death of the Lord? Once a year the Jewish Passover recalled the great delivering action of the God of Israel; should Christians follow that pattern?[35] In a sense John answers those questions. The eucharistic teaching comes as a commentary on the multiplication of the loaves and thus is intimately related to what Jesus did in his ministry. The eucharist is not explicitly

[35] Interestingly in the Roman Catholic liturgy only one Mass is designated as the celebration of the Lord's Supper, namely, the Mass celebrated on Holy Thursday.

Brief Reflections on John 3 and John 6

related to Jesus' death but is treated as food, the bread of life, and thus should be received frequently.

Chapter 6 begins with the multiplication of the loaves and the walking on the water, a combined scene in which John is substantially close to the Synoptic account(s). There is an echo of the miracles of Moses during the exodus (manna, walking dryshod through the sea), but John's young lad with barley loaves heightens the secondary similarity to the Elijah/Elisha miracle pattern (II Kings 4:42-44). The peculiarly Johannine contribution comes the next day when implicitly the evangelist answers the intriguing question that haunts readers of the Synoptics: What happened to those people for whom Jesus worked miracles? Did the miracle change their lives? Did they become believers?

John indicates that those for whom the bread was multiplied really saw no profound significance beyond that it was a good way to get bread. While John certainly thought that there was a multiplication of physical loaves, he now has to make clear that the Son of Man who has come down from above did not do so to satisfy physical hunger. People who have loaves multiplied for them will become physically hungry again; he has come to give a heavenly bread that people will eat and never again become hungry. In 4:14 Jesus spoke to the Samaritan woman of his ability to give water that people would drink and never thirst again, and here the Johannine Jesus is completing the picture of eternal food and drink. In discussing John 3, I explained that the Gospel employs the imagery of a birth from above that gives eternal life even as birth from parents gives earthly life. Once born, those with earthly life have to take physical food and drink to remain alive; once born, those with eternal life have to take eternal food and drink to remain alive.

Jesus' remarks on the bread of life, we are finally told (6:59), were given in a synagogue; and indeed we can understand the sermon better if we know how homilies were composed at this period. The basic pattern was a detailed

Chapter 2: The Jerusalem Church of One Mind

exposition of a passage from the Pentateuch of Moses illustrated by a supporting passage from the Prophets. In debating with him about what he had done in multiplying loaves and what importance he had, the crowd supplies the biblical text, "He gave them bread from heaven to eat" (John 6:31; see Exod 16:4, 15) which they interpret as: Moses gave our ancestors the manna to eat. (Once again, as in chapter 3, the dignity of Jesus will be made clear by comparison with Moses.) Jesus denies their interpretation: The "He" is the heavenly Father not Moses; the tense of the verb is "gives," not "gave";[36] and the bread from heaven is not the manna because those who ate that bread died. The true bread is Jesus who comes down from heaven so that people may eat and never die.

Already in the Old Testament God's revelation (specifically the Law) was compared to a well of water and to food, and people were warned that it is not by physical bread alone that they live but by every word that comes from the mouth of God. In that vein Jesus first presents himself as the bread of life come down from heaven in the sense of embodying divine revelation that people must believe (6:35, 40; notice that in 6:35-50 there is little emphasis on eating the bread of life).[37] The prophetic quotation that supports Jesus' exegesis is "They shall all be taught by God" (6:45; from Isaiah 54:13), which is literally true since Jesus who is doing this teaching is the Word-become-flesh, and "the Word was God." The "Jews" murmur at him (even as their ancestors murmured at Moses in the desert): Jesus cannot have come down from heaven because they know his parents. As with Nicodemus this reflects a misunderstanding on the part of those who

[36] The exegesis behind this particular point seems to be based on the ability to read a form of Hebrew *ntn* (the root for "give") as either a past indicative or a present participle.

[37] I am deliberately simplifying by stressing revelation as the main theme in 6:35-50 and the eucharist as the main theme in 6:51-58. The interweaving is more complicated.

Brief Reflections on John 3 and John 6

think on an earthly level; the parent of whom Jesus is speaking is the heavenly Father.

In 6:51-58 the bread of life takes on another dimension as the language shifts to eating and drinking, to flesh and blood. "The bread that I shall give is my flesh for the life of the world" is quite close to the Lucan Last Supper declaration, "This is my body which is given for you,"[38] and may well have been the Johannine eucharistic formula. To this there is another Jewish objection, parallel to the one in the first part of the discourse, as if Jesus was offering his tangible flesh in a cannibalistic way. But Jesus insists that his flesh is truly food and his blood truly drink (not on a crassly carnal level, of course: 6:63).

Acts has told us of the eucharistic breaking of the bread as an element in Christian *koinōnia*; John in a poetic way has laid out for us the basic elements that can make the Christian eucharistic celebration nourishing. If the service of the word feeds us with divine revelation as the bread of life, and the service of the sacrament feeds us with the flesh and blood of Christ, the life with which we are endowed at baptism will remain.

[38] An underlying Semitic *bŝr* was rendered more literally in some Greek-speaking communities as *sarx* ("flesh") and more idiomatically in others as *sōma* ("body").

Chapter 2: The Jerusalem Church of One Mind

Chapter 3

Diversity in the Jerusalem Church; Expansion to Judea and Samaria (Acts 6-9)

After the Sanhedrin session at which Gamaliel spoke (*ca.* AD 36?), Acts begins an era in which, except for the brief period in which a Jewish king ruled Judea (Herod Agrippa I; AD 41-44; Acts 12:1-23), the branch of the Jerusalem church closely associated with the Twelve was not persecuted.[39] That period would come to an end in AD 62 when James, the brother of the Lord and leader of the Jerusalem church, was put to death.[40] Thus, according to the implicit indications of Acts, for some twenty years (AD 36-40, 45-62) the main Christian leaders could have functioned with Jerusalem as a base without attempts by the Jewish authorities to have them exterminated. This is not implausible, for we have indications that Paul could go to Jerusalem within those years and see some of the "pillars of the church" without any indication of secrecy. However, the removal of the external threat did not mean that all was well. Suddenly, after speaking of the church as being of one mind, at the beginning of chapter 6 Acts tells us about a hostile division among Jerusalem Christians, a division that will bring persecution on a segment of them (not those closely associated with the apostles) and lead eventually to a great missionary enterprise.

---

[39] To forestall an objection, let me point out that the Hellenist branch of the Jerusalem church (e.g., Stephen) was persecuted; but Acts 8:1 maintains that in that persecution and expulsion the "apostles" were not bothered, and for Acts "apostles" refers to the Twelve (exception 14:14).

[40] This James, who was not one of the Twelve, was closely connected with them, whether or not Luke would have considered him an apostle. For Paul "apostle" was a wider term and included (besides himself) a major figure like James of Jerusalem (Galatians 1:19).

Selections from this section of Acts serve as Lectionary readings on three weekdays at the end of the 2d Week of Easter and the beginning of the 3d Week; and on two Sundays (5th, 7th, A and C respectively).

Acts 6:1-6: Divisive Behavior within the Jerusalem Church. Probably here Acts draws on an old tradition, and the account is sketchy. (Was the source sketchy or did the author choose not to dwell on such an unpleasantry in a church that he has told us was of one mind?) The division manifests itself in an area that Acts has lauded several times: the common goods. Now, however, this feature is no longer a sign of *koinōnia*, for two groups of Jewish believers within the Jerusalem community are fighting over the common goods. Why? The designation of one group as Hellenists (Greek-like) and the Greek names of their leaders (6:5) suggest that they were Jews (in one case a proselyte or convert to Judaism) who spoke (only?) Greek and who were raised as children acculturated to Greco-Roman civilization. Deductively by contrast, then, the other group called the Hebrews would have spoken Aramaic or Hebrew (sometimes as well as Greek) and have been more culturally Jewish in outlook.[41] Beyond the cultural difference apparently there was also a theological difference. The apostles, who were clearly Hebrew Christians, did not let their faith in Jesus stop them from worshipping in the Temple (Acts 2:46; 3:1; 5:12, 21). However, Stephen, who will become the Hellenist leader, speaks as if the Temple has no more meaning (7:48-50). In fact, we know that Jews of this period were sharply divided over the claim that the Jerusalem Temple was the sole place on earth at which sacrifice

[41] Paul, who probably knew Hebrew or Aramaic as well as Greek, considered himself a Hebrew (II Corinthians 11:22; Philippians 3:5) in his strict preconversional behavior as a Jew, whether or not that designation meant the same to him as it did to the author of Acts.

Chapter 3: The Jerusalem Church, Diversity and Expansion

could be offered to God; and so it is not improbable that Jews of opposite persuasion on that issue may have become believers in Jesus. Some of them would have regarded that faith as a catalyst toward the demise of the importance of Temple cult. In any case the disagreement among these Jerusalem Christians has been translated into finances (as have many inner church fights ever since) because the Hebrews (surely the larger group) were attempting to force the Hellenists to conformity by shutting off common funds from the Hellenist widows, who presumably were totally dependent on this support.

In order to deal with this situation the Twelve summoned "the multitude" of the disciples (perhaps a technical name for those who could vote) to settle the issue. In this session the Twelve avoided the obvious, simple solutions. Although Hebrews themselves, they did not simply side with the Hebrews and demand that the Hellenists either conform or leave. Moreover, they refused to take over the administration of the common goods; specifically they did not wish to involve themselves in waiting on or serving[42] tables in order to ensure a fair distribution of food. Rather they wished to allow the Hellenists to have their own leaders and administrators of the common goods.

This brief scene offers Christians of today important subjects for reflection. First, nowhere do we see more clearly the unique role of the Twelve.[43] A symbolic group at the begin-

---

[42] Because the verb "to wait on, serve" in Acts 6:2 is *diakonein*, this scene has come to be interpreted as the establishment of the first deacons. The position of the Hellenist leaders who are selected in this scene is not similar to that of the deacons described in the Pastoral Letters. If one wants to be anachronistic and apply a later ecclesiastical term to their role, these administrators would be closer to bishops than to deacons.

[43] It needs to be emphasized that in the total New Testament picture "the Twelve" and "apostles" are not simply equatable terms even though the Twelve were also apostles. The apostles (a larger group than the Twelve as the distinction in I Corinthians 15:5, 7 makes lucidly clear when it distinguishes between "the Twelve" and "all the apostles") are commissioned to

ning of the renewed Israel (even as the twelve sons of Jacob/Israel were esteemed as the originators of the twelve tribes), the Twelve have the eschatological function of purifying and maintaining the wholeness of God's people. They are once and for all, never replaced; there are only twelve thrones of judgment and they are to have them. Here the concern of the Twelve for the whole of the renewed Israel is exemplified in their refusing to take a partisan position. They preserve the *koinōnia* by their solution, for the Hellenists are to remain as fully recognized brothers and sisters in Christ. Peter is normally the spokesman of the Twelve, and in the church today the symbolic functioning of the Twelve is represented by the successor of Peter when the papacy is at its best. There are always factions in the church who want their opponents excommunicated or suppressed because they are not "true Catholics" or "true Christians." But the successor of Peter, who symbolizes the unity of the whole people of God, has as a principal task to hold the *koinōnia* together. One of his great glories is to keep people in the church and not let them be driven out.

Second, in reality the acceptance of the suggestion made by the Twelve was a decision in the early church for pluralism and an appropriation of what we have come to call today "the hierarchy of doctrine." The cultural and theological differences that existed in Jerusalem between the Hebrews and the Hellenists were implicitly being judged as less important than their common belief in Jesus. That same instinct will manifest itself later when it comes to the issue of whether circumcised believers can accept uncircumcised believers as equally and truly Christian. From the beginning Christianity has not gloried in uniformity except in basics,

---

proclaim the risen Lord and gather believers. In the traditional theology bishops are "successors of the apostles" (not "successors of the Twelve" as such) because they inherit the care of the churches that emerged from the apostolic mission.

Chapter 3: The Jerusalem Church, Diversity and Expansion

e.g., the christological identity of Jesus as uniquely embodying God's presence. Most believers in Jesus decided very early that it was better to tolerate differences of practices and of theological attitudes rather than to destroy the *koinōnia*.

Third, the scene illustrates certain factors about the nature and origins of church structure. No blueprint had come from Jesus showing how the community of those who believed in him was to be administered. By the time described in Acts 6 (*ca.* AD 36?) believers are increasing in numbers and are arguing with one another—two sociological factors that always produce a need for defining leadership more clearly. The Twelve refuse to become administrators for local groups; yet such administrators now need to be appointed. Accordingly we hear of the seven who become the administrators for the Hellenist believers. Probably administrators also emerge for the Hebrew Christian community at the same time; henceforth (Acts 11:30; 12:17; 15:2, 4, 6, 13, 22, 23; 21:18) James the brother of the Lord and the elders (presbyters) shall appear as authorities in Jerusalem, alongside the apostles. The choice of administrators in 6:6 is done in the context of praying and the laying on of hands. Too often when modern Christians think of church structure, they take a simple, not to say simplistic, view. On the ultraliberal end of the Christian spectrum, church structure is seen simply as a sociological development that can be changed by voting. On the ultraconservative end of the spectrum church structure is seen to have been established by Jesus and no changes are permissible. Precisely because Jesus did not leave blueprints, church structure developed to meet needs; and so sociological factors have played a role. Yet in Christian self-understanding the Holy Spirit given by the risen Christ guided the church in the way it developed, so that structure came to embody Jesus Christ's will for his church. (For that reason, certain basic aspects of the structure are believed by Christians to be unchangeable.) In other words, on the analogy of the incarnation, there is both the human and the divine in the church

Diversity and Its Effects

and its structure. A recognition of that will allow adaptations in church structure to meet the needs of our day without giving us the sense that each generation is free to reinvent the church.

Fourth, as depicted in Acts the Twelve made a good proposal—"the multitude" of the Jerusalem community recognized that by expressing approval. Nevertheless, as we are about to see, the decision had unexpected results that caused those in authority in Jerusalem many problems. Certainly none of those present at this meeting could have foreseen how far their decision would lead the church. (We should always recognize that with any major decision in the church the results are likely to go beyond what was foreseen and that often there is no way to stop at a point we judge prudent the thrust of what we have begun.) Let us now look at the aftermath.

Acts 6:7–7:60: Effects of Keeping the Hellenists within the Christian Communion. In keeping the Hellenists within the Christian *koinōnia* the Jerusalem community now becomes responsible for the actions and preaching of the Hellenist leaders. The chief priests and the Sanhedrin had implicitly decided to extend grudging tolerance to those who believed in the risen Christ (even though technically they were forbidden to speak in the name of Jesus); but that did not mean they would tolerate attacks on the Temple from believers in Jesus any more than they tolerated it from other Jews.[44] The first-ranking among the Hellenists, Stephen, stirs up opposition at a Jerusalem synagogue attended largely by foreign Jews. They drag him before a Sanhedrin and level a charge about the message he is preaching—not that Jesus is risen (the previous issue that had disturbed the Sanhedrin about

---

[44] The Jewish writer Josephus speaks of various sects of the Jews (Sadducees, Pharisees, Essenes); and presumably the believers of Jesus would have been considered another, annoying variety, even if they did not think of themselves in this category (Acts 24:14).

Chapter 3: The Jerusalem Church, Diversity and Expansion

the Twelve), but that Jesus would destroy the Temple. Interestingly, although in the trial of Jesus Mark and Matthew had false witnesses charge Jesus with saying that he would destroy the Temple sanctuary (Mark: "made with hands"), Luke omitted that charge against Jesus. Did the evangelist want to lead his readers to a more subtle understanding, namely, that what was destructive to the Temple in Jesus' proclamation became apparent only after his lifetime and then through those believers, like the Hellenists, who saw the more radical implications of Jesus' message?[45] In his long speech (Acts 7:2-53) in response to the Temple charge Stephen will phrase those radical implications in the climactic statement: "The Most High does not dwell in houses made with hands" (7:48).

Although Acts gives us speeches of Peter and Paul, none is so grand as the speech of Stephen. Is that because the Christianity that exists in the author's lifetime has now followed the path of Stephen in terms of rejection of the Temple rather than that of Peter and Paul, both of whom are described as worshiping in the Temple? Stephen's survey of the salvation history from the patriarch Abraham to Israel's entrance into the Promised Land under Moses and Joshua has fascinated scholars since elements in it do not seem to reflect standard Old Testament understanding. Some have even proposed that we have here reflections of a Samaritan background harmonious with the mission in Samaria that will soon be undertaken by the Hellenists. That discussion is too technical for our interests here, especially since only the

[45] We are uncertain of the logic because the charge against Stephen in Acts 6:13 (as against Jesus in Mark and Matthew) is attributed to false witnesses. Why are the witnesses called false? Since the finale of Stephen's defense speech seems to offer a basis for accusing him of opposition toward the Temple and having radical ideas about the Law, it is unlikely that we are meant to think that the witnesses simply invented the charge. Perhaps they may have oversimplified the causality as if Jesus (or some of the Christians) planned personally to do physical damage to the Temple.

Diversity and Its Effects

last three verses of the speech (7:51-53) are read in the postEaster Lectionary. Those verses are astoundingly polemic from a prisoner in the dock, for Stephen accuses his hearers of giving over and murdering Jesus the just one even as their fathers persecuted the prophets. Not surprisingly this accusation brings the rage against Stephen to the boiling point, and he is cast out of the city and stoned to death (7:54-60). Both the Sunday and weekday Lectionaries contain the account of this death; and the scene is truly significant, not only because Stephen is the first Christian martyr, but also because the death of Stephen in Acts matches so closely the death of Jesus in Luke. Both accounts speak of the Son of Man (standing/seated) at the right hand of God (Luke 22:69; Acts 7:56); both have a prayer for the forgiveness of those who are effecting this execution (Luke 23:34; Acts 7:60); both have the dying figure commend his spirit heavenward (Luke 23:46; Acts 7:59). In the figure of Peter Acts has shown continuity with Jesus' ministry of healing and preaching; in the figure of Stephen Acts has shown continuity with Jesus' death. And just as Jesus' death was not the end because the apostles would receive his Spirit to carry on the work, the death of Stephen is not the end, for observing is a young man named Saul (7:58). He consents to the death (8:1), but in God's providence he will continue the work of Stephen.

EXPANSION TO JUDEA AND SAMARIA;
HELLENIST MISSION; CONVERSION OF SAUL;
PETER'S ACTIVITIES (ACTS 8:1–9:43)
Selections from this section of Acts serve as Lectionary readings on four weekdays at the end of the 3d Week of Easter; and on two Sundays (5th, 6th, B and A respectively).

Acts 8:1-40: The Hellenist Mission. In a complicated description that involves the phrase "all were scattered," Acts 8:1 now tells us that a selective persecution followed the death of Stephen. The Hellenists were scattered; the apostles (and

Chapter 3: The Jerusalem Church, Diversity and Expansion

seemingly the Hebrew Christians) were not, presumably because they did not propagandize against the Temple as the Hellenists did. In this persecution a ferocious agent is Saul whose conversion will be dramatically recounted in the next chapter. Acts 1:8 laid out the divine plan of evangelization: "You shall be my witnesses in Jerusalem and in all Judea and Samaria, and to the ends of the earth."[46] We have heard of witness (*martyria*) borne in Jerusalem culminating with the martyrdom of Stephen; now we are to hear about preaching in the next two regions as the Hellenists are scattered throughout Judea and Samaria. The picture of the spread of Christianity is highly selective; in 9:2, 10 we shall find a reference to Christian believers in Damascus without being told how they got there! Nevertheless it is interesting to reflect on the simplified picture in Acts 8.

First, such a basic step as moving outside Jerusalem to preach to a wider audience is not the result of planning but of persecution. Aspects of that picture will be true of many new missions throughout the ages: External pressure will cause Christians to see an area or means of evangelization that would not have occurred to them, and occasionally a harsh disaster will be turned into an opportunity. Thus once again Acts shows us that from the very start Christianity was not governed by a blueprint but by the Spirit.

Second, those who are expelled and become the missionaries to areas outside Jerusalem are the Hellenists, the more radical Christians in terms of their relation to Jewish Temple worship. Missionary activity in itself might have been neutral

[46] Acts presents these as the risen Jesus' words; but that must be understood correctly, for the book goes on to show that the disciples had no awareness that they had been informed of such a plan. In terms of origin most scholars would think that the material available to the author of Acts, writing some fifty years after the early evangelizing, enabled him to detect a geographical expansion; and he has used that expansion as a plan for the book. He would have looked on this procedure as discovering what Christ had willed for his church, whence the attribution of it to the risen Jesus.

Expansion to Judea and Samaria

in the attitude it inculcated toward Judaism, but with the Hellenists as spokesmen it was bound to have a centrifugal force. Their converts to Jesus would have no deep attachment to features of Jewish worship; and where they encountered opposition from Jews who did not believe in Jesus, they would have felt less obligated to preserve a Christian attachment to the Jewish synagogues.

Third, the Hellenists, who differed from Hebrews (whether or not the latter had come to faith in Jesus), seemingly felt less obligated to preach Jesus only or even chiefly to Jews. Acts 8:5 tells us they went to the Samaritans; and 11:19-20 indicates that in Phoenica, Cyprus, and Antioch, although at first they spoke the word only to Jews, some preached to Gentiles. The instinct to go to Samaria is interesting. One of the major differences between Samaritans and Jews was that the former did not accept the Jerusalem Temple as the only place of worship. Since the Christian Hellenists were Jews who did not believe that God dwelt in houses made with hands, they were ideally suited to preach Jesus Christ to an area that might well have been hostile to Hebrew Christians who kept going to the Temple. (Many think that there is a Hellenist strain in John, the only Gospel where Jesus goes into Samaria and gains Samaritan followers. In John 4:21 we may be hearing the type of preaching done in Samaria by the Hellenists, for it speaks of an hour "when you will worship the Father neither on this mountain [Gerizim, the Samaritan holy place] nor in Jerusalem.")

In any case the Hellenist proclamation of the good news to the Samaritans is highly successful. Yet the net of proclamation attracts Simon Magus, a figure who later became a subject of speculation, figuring in legend as the great adversary of Christianity. Does the author of Acts include the story of his defeat because already when Acts was being written gnostics were active who made Simon a hero?[47] Interestingly

[47] The designation of Simon as "the Power of God called Great" sounds

Chapter 3: The Jerusalem Church, Diversity and Expansion

the one to confront Simon is Peter, not Philip the Hellenist successor of Stephen. The Jerusalem church has heard of the Hellenist success and sent Peter and John that they might receive the Holy Spirit. (One suspects that this is bowdlerizing the basic purpose of the apostolic visitation, namely, to verify whether the conversion of such outsiders as the Samaritans is reconcilable with Jesus' proclamation.) The impression is created in Acts that granting the Spirit required the collaborative presence of the Twelve. Simon wants their power and offers money for it (thus forever immortalizing his name in the designation "simony"). Peter challenges him to repent; yet unlike Stephen's prayer for his adversaries, this promotion of repentance is qualified as to whether Simon can really change his heart (8:22-23). That qualification may have fed the later legends. The experience in Samaria is pictured as influencing Peter and John because on their way back to Jerusalem they preached the gospel to Samaritans (8:25).

Acts 8:26-40 supplies another example of Hellenist evangelization, this time in the southern part of Judea rather than the north, again manifesting geographical spread. The fact that the Ethiopian eunuch has come to Jerusalem to worship and is reading Isaiah gives the impression of a foreign Jew from an exotic region in Africa (one of "the ends of the earth," whether modern Ethiopia or Nubia to the south of Egypt is envisaged). Philip the Hellenist's ability to interpret the prophet in order to explain Christ to the eunuch is a continuation of the risen Jesus' interpreting the Scriptures for his disciples (Luke 24:27, 44-45). Deuteronomy 23:2(1) would rule out the admission of the castrated into the community of Israel, but Philip has no hesitation about meeting the eunuch's request to be baptized into the community of the renewed Israel. That openness prepares us for the admission of

---

as if he was one of the gnostic emanations that stand between the distant, hidden God and human beings. Is the author's categorizing him as a *magus* a contemptuous classification of a gnostic teacher?

Expansion to Judea and Samaria

Gentiles, and by way of transition Acts stops here to tell us about Saul/Paul who would be the great emissary to the Gentiles.

Acts 9:1-30: The Conversion of Saul. Besides narrating the account of the conversion here, the author will report it twice more from Paul's lips in his speeches of self-defense (22:3-21; 26:2-23).[48] In those later versions the vocation of Paul to evangelize the Gentiles will be blended into the conversion account. Here the author is content to move in stages: Ananias who cures and baptizes him is told of the future mission, but not Saul himself. Yet clearly it is because of all that is to be accomplished through this "vessel of election" (9:15) that Acts is so interested in recounting his dramatic conversion effected by Jesus himself.[49] The dramatic touches of the story are superb, e.g., the personalizing of Saul's hostility in 9:4, "Saul, Saul, why do you persecute me?" The reluctance of Ananias to have anything to do with Saul despite the Lord's instruction highlights the metamorphosis of Saul from a truly fearsome persecutor. Acts is very careful to report that this great missionary received the Holy Spirit (9:17); for his proclamation will eventually be as potent as was that of Peter and the others who received the Spirit at Pentecost. In chapter 1 above I wrote about the importance of christological belief; in significant harmony with that Acts sums up the new convert's preaching as "Jesus is the Son of God" (9:20). Acts also lays the basis for the future activity of Barnabas with Paul by telling us that it was Barnabas who supported

[48] Only the first of the three is read in the Lectionary of this season between Easter and Pentecost.

[49] The risen Jesus appeared on earth to the Twelve and then departed to heaven whence he now speaks to Saul. Does that mean that the author of Acts posits a qualitative difference of status between the Twelve and Paul in terms of their relationship to Christ? I Corinthians 15:5-8, from Paul himself, would give the impression that there was no difference in the appearances of the risen Jesus to Peter or the Twelve and the appearance to Paul (other than time: they are listed first, he is last).

Chapter 3: The Jerusalem Church, Diversity and Expansion

Saul against those in Jerusalem who could not believe that the persecutor had now changed. Evidently under the constraint of actual history, Acts postpones the most famous activities of Saul/Paul by telling us that he went back to Tarsus (9:30); his great mission will be described later after the author tells us more about Peter.[50]

Acts 9:31-43: Peter's Activities. The first of the Twelve was the spokesman of apostolic missionary activity in Jerusalem (Acts 2–5); now that the church has been spreading to Judea and Samaria[51] the Hellenists and Saul have taken center stage (with Peter invoked chiefly to face Simon Magus). Beginning in 9:31, however, Peter returns to the fore, first for his missionary work in Lydda and Joppa and then (10:1ff.) for his pivotal role in bringing Gentiles into the *koinōnia*. (The first element really prepares for the second.) Previously we have seen that in the name of Jesus Peter could heal and preach. Acts now reiterates this parallelism, for the cure of Aeneas at Lydda with the command to rise echoes closely Jesus' cure of the paralyzed man (Luke 5:24-26). Even more closely the revivification of Tabitha resembles Jesus' action in raising the daughter of Jairus (Luke 8:49-56).[52] No power has been withheld from the church, not even the power over death itself. Now, however, we are about to move beyond the parallels to Jesus' ministry to a new area, the Gentiles. The Lucan Gospel account of Jesus began and ended in the Jerusalem Temple. What Peter does next will eventually take Christianity outside Judaism to Rome as representative of the ends of the earth.

[50] The overlapping of the two figures helps to show that the same gospel was preached by both.

[51] Having listed Judea and Samaria as the next stage after Jerusalem in 1:8, the author of Acts is careful to signpost that geographical expansion (chapters 8–9) by mentioning Judea and Samaria in 8:1 and 9:31.

[52] The order "Tabitha, rise" in Acts 9:40 is remarkably like "*Talitha cum(i)*" in the parallel Marcan account (5:41).

Expansion to Judea and Samaria

Brief Reflections on John 10 and John 12

In the week (the 4th of Easter) just after the Lectionary offers selections from Acts 6–9, its Gospel selections are from John 10 and 12.[53] We saw in Acts 6 how a divided community created the need for an administrative leadership, and how persecution drove the Hellenists out of Jerusalem to begin a mission to the Samaritan outsiders. It is quite appropriate, then, to turn to Gospel readings from John that deal with shepherding the flock and other sheep not of this fold.

Structures of authority developed gradually in the early church. Shortly after the selection of local administrators for the Hellenist Christians, James and the elders are portrayed as the leaders of the Jerusalem Hebrew Christian community. Acts 14:23 has Paul appointing presbyters in the churches, and 20:28 has him tell the presbyters of Ephesus to shepherd the flock in which the Holy Spirit has made them overseers. Reading John against that background supplies an interesting corrective of the long-term dangers inherent in such structuring. Figures given authority in the church tend to become all important in the eyes of those whom they were meant to serve; their presence is immediate, and often it seems that Jesus is reached chiefly through them and their activities. For John the immediacy of Jesus is crucially important because only he can give God's life. At the end of the 1st century when the language of shepherds was widespread for those in charge of churches, the Johannine insistence that Jesus is the good or model shepherd and that all others are thieves and bandits is challenging. The sheep should heed only the divine shepherd. True, in the Johannine context the words are addressed to the Jews and so the primary attack may be on the leadership of the synagogues, but such language is bound to have a dynamism in making Christians qualify the role of their own leaders.

[53] The 4th Sunday of Easter, where the readings in all three cycles are from John 10, is sometimes called Good Shepherd Sunday.

Chapter 3: The Jerusalem Church, Diversity and Expansion

Later in John 21:15-17 we see a shepherding role of feeding the sheep entrusted to Simon Peter, a human being; but even then the sheep are not his—only Jesus can call them "my sheep." The shepherding image in the Old Testament is sometimes used to symbolize the ruling power of the king. Yet Jesus as the model shepherd does not speak of his authority or of ruling. He speaks of his intimate knowledge of his sheep and of an ability to call each by name so that they will recognize him when he leads them to pasture. Jesus speaks also of his willingness to lay down his life for the sheep lest they be snatched by the wolf. This is what makes shepherding truly pastoral. Accordingly, in chapter 21 when Simon Peter is appointed to feed the sheep, Jesus signifies how Peter will die a martyr's death, a death that qualifies him as a shepherd according to the good shepherd's standards. Thus, while for a church that has strongly articulated structure Acts supplies evidence of that necessary development as early as apostolic times, John offers a critique that helps to insure that structure does not interfere with an immediate relationship between Jesus and the believers that is at the heart of Christianity.

John 10:16 indicates that Jesus has other sheep that are not of this fold and that he wishes to bring them into the one flock under the one shepherd. Most likely, given the distinctiveness that surrounds the beloved disciple (the model of the Johannine community) in the Fourth Gospel, and the constant contrast between that disciple and Simon Peter, the Johannine community was not entirely one with churches that considered the Twelve as their patrons—a situation that has some similarity to the difficult relationship between the Hebrew and Hellenist Christians in Acts. On the importance of the *koinōnia* or oneness of the church both Acts and John agree. As indicated in reflections above, this ideal remains of paramount importance for relationships not only among the Christian churches but even within a church like the Roman Catholic. The tendency to divide over issues must be con-

Brief Reflections on John 10 and John 12

fronted by the stated demand of Jesus to be the one shepherd over the one flock.

As we judge what is essential for unity and what are tolerable diversities, we must come back to the criterion of christology put forth by Peter in Acts when he insisted on baptism in the name of Jesus, i.e., the confession of who Jesus is. There are other essential Christian beliefs, but they must be evaluated by their interrelationship with the all-essential belief in Christ. That is harmonious with the weekday Lectionary passage John 12:44-50 where Jesus states that those who believe in him are really believing in the God who sent him and that judgment will be based on such faith. Those who see Jesus and refuse belief are judging themselves. The majority of people in the world today are not Christians: They do not believe in Jesus, and indeed many can be said not to have seen him. They have their own struggle with light and darkness, and their salvation is entrusted to the all-gracious God whose ultimate goal is salvific (see 12:47). As for Christians, as we seek the grace to constitute the one flock under the one shepherd, our immediate concern must be for our fellow believers—to be sure that the faith we profess in Christ is what is demanded in Acts and John.

Chapter 3: The Jerusalem Church, Diversity and Expansion

Chapter 4

Outreach to the Gentiles;
The Church of Antioch (Acts 10-14)

Gradually the author of Acts shifts attention to the mission to the Gentiles. In chapter 10 Peter is led by the Spirit to baptize Cornelius (and his household), a pious God-fearer, i.e., a Gentile who participates in synagogue prayers and accepts the moral demands of Judaism. In 11:20 we are told that the Hellenists began preaching to the Greek-speaking Gentiles. In 13:4ff. the mission of Barnabas and Saul from Antioch is described, a mission that first preaches to the Jews in the synagogues but gradually turns to the Gentiles.

THE CONVERSION OF THE GENTILE CORNELIUS
(ACTS 10:1–11:18)

In Acts 10 the author as a third-person reporter recounts what happened; in Acts 11 Peter in his own first-person report repeats what happened as he defends his behavior before the Jerusalem Christians. (As with Paul's repetitions of the story of his conversion, the duplication signals that this is an account of pivotal importance.) Selections from the first part of this section are read on the B Sunday of the 6th Week of Easter, while 11:1-18 is read on the Monday of the 4th Week of Easter. In other words the Lectionary is satisfied with an overall impression of what was involved. Actually there are six subdivisions in the Acts narrative: (a) 10:1-8: The pious Roman centurion Cornelius receives a vision of an angel of God at Caesarea telling him to send to Joppa for Simon called Peter; (b) 10:9-16: At Joppa Peter receives a vision telling him that foods traditionally considered ritually unclean are in fact not unclean; (c) 10:17-23a: Pondering the vision, Peter receives the men sent by Cornelius who ask him to come to Cornelius' house; (d) 10:23b-33: Cornelius

The Conversion of the Gentile Cornelius

receives Peter and explains that he was told to send for him; (e) 10:34-49: Peter preaches a sermon, and the Holy Spirit comes upon the uncircumcised present, so that Peter commands them to be baptized; (f) 11:1-18: Returning to Jerusalem, Peter has to account for his boldness in baptizing Gentiles.[54]

Because there are heavenly revelations both to Cornelius and Peter, readers are meant to recognize that what occurs here is uniquely God's will. Such an emphasis was probably necessary because of the controversial nature of the two issues involved: Were Christians bound by the Jewish rules for kosher foods? Should the Gentiles be received without first becoming Jews (i.e., being circumcised)? The postEaster Lectionary ignores the former, perhaps because those who shaped the Lectionary did not think the issue of enduring import. Yet here we have a major break from Jewish practice, a break supported not by a Hellenist radical but by the first of the Twelve. Gradually the extent to which new wine cannot be put into old wine skins (Luke 5:37) is becoming apparent. Often modern Jewish and Christian scholars, studying the history of this early period and regretting the great rift that opened between Christianity and Judaism, suggest that if in the 1st century there had been more tolerance and understanding on both sides, the split could have been avoided. Some indications in the New Testament, however, suggest that the radical implications of Jesus were really irreconcilable with major tenets and practices of Judaism.

Lectionary (and indeed general Christian) attention is focused on the second issue: Did Gentiles have to be circumcised to receive baptism and the grace of Christ? Notice that the issue concerns Gentiles. So far as I know the New Testament does not debate whether Jewish Christian parents should have their sons circumcised. Not even Paul, who

---

[54] The Lectionary in concerned with small portions of (d) and (e) and the whole of (f).

Chapter 4: Outreach to the Gentiles

faces over and over again this issue with the Gentiles, ever states explicitly what a Jewish Christian should do. I would assume that most Jewish Christians did (and should have) circumcised their sons in order to continue to receive the special privileges of being Jews. That would have become problematic theologically only if they thought that circumcision was necessary along with baptism for someone to become a child of God and part of God's people newly chosen in Jesus Christ.

Implicitly or explicitly those who insisted that Gentiles needed to be circumcised (i.e., become Jews) were maintaining that being a Jew had primacy over faith in Christ in terms of God's grace. Peter is pictured as rejecting that in his speech and action in 10:34-49. Scholars debate whether the author of Acts is historical in presenting Peter as the first to accept uncircumcised Gentiles into the Christian *koinōnia*. One may argue from 11:20 that the Hellenists were the first to do this, and clearly later Paul was the greatest spokesman for the practice. Yet since Paul mentions Peter (or Kephas) at Antioch dealing with Gentiles (Galatians 2:11-12) and at Corinth (I Corinthians 9:5), what may underlie Acts is the memory that among the Jerusalem leaders Peter was foremost in displaying such openness, whence the ability of Peter or his image to appeal to both sides of the Christian community.[55] From what is described here, we may reflect on several issues of relevance to Christians today.

First, as incredible as it may seem, such a fundamental issue as whether one should proclaim the kingdom to Gentiles and whether they had to become Jews was not detectably an issue solved by Jesus in his lifetime.[56] There are those today

[55] Paul (Galatians 2:7) speaks of Peter's having been entrusted with the gospel to the circumcised; yet a letter attributed to him, I Peter, is clearly written to Gentile Christians (2:10: "You were once no people").

[56] The stories of the Syro-Phoenician woman who asked to have her daughter healed and of the Roman centurion whose faith Jesus praised are of exceptional character and do not really settle the problem.

The Conversion of the Gentile Cornelius

on both extremes of the ecclesiastical spectrum (ultraliberal, ultraconservative) who think they can appeal to the words or deeds of Jesus to solve any question in the church (parochial, diocesan, or universal). If Jesus did not solve the most fundamental question of the Christian mission, we may well doubt that his recorded words solve most of our subsequent debated problems in the church.

Second, Peter is not presented as solving the problem by his own initiative or wisdom. He says in Acts 10:28 that God has shown him that he should not consider others unclean. Moreover, from the fact that Cornelius has received a vision from God Peter concludes that God shows no partiality (10:34). The reason Peter offers for not forbidding the uncircumcised Cornelius to be baptized is that the Holy Spirit has come upon him (10:47).[57] In other words we have another instance of Christians facing an unforeseen problem and solving it, not by appeal to a previous blueprint for the church, but by insight (gained from the Holy Spirit) as to what Christ wanted for the church.

Third, the radical character of what Peter has done and proclaimed is challenged in 11:3 by confreres in the church of Jerusalem: "Why did you go to the uncircumcised and eat with them?" It is not clear whether at heart this Christian "circumcision party" was altogether opposed to converting Gentiles to belief in Christ or was simply insisting that Gentiles could be converted only after they had become Jews.[58]

---

[57] Some today would try to solve a modern issue about "baptism in the Spirit" (as distinct from baptism in water) from the sequence in Acts. That is not possible. According to his purpose and interests the author of Acts shows: (a) the Twelve and those together with them receiving the Spirit without (ever) being baptized in water; (b) people being baptized (in water) and then receiving the gift of the Spirit (2:38; 19:5-6); (c) people receiving the Spirit before being baptized in water (here); (d) people having been baptized in water (with the baptism of John) who never even knew that there was a Holy Spirit (18:24–19:7).

[58] Similarly, as we shall see, among those Jewish Christians open to converting Gentiles to Christ without demanding circumcision there were differ-

Chapter 4: Outreach to the Gentiles

One may imagine this group appealing to Abraham and Moses as proof that the Scriptures demanded circumcision and arguing there was no evidence that Jesus had ever changed the requirement for circumcision.[59] Peter answers the circumcision party by telling about his visions and the coming of the Spirit upon Cornelius' household. This existential argument silences the circumcision party (for the moment) and leads to the acceptance of Gentiles into existing Jewish Christian groups (11:18). But the issue has not been fully resolved, as Acts will show us after it has depicted an active mission to Gentiles.

DEVELOPMENTS AT ANTIOCH AND JERUSALEM (ACTS 11:19–12:25)

(From this section only what happens at Antioch is narrated in the Lectionary, in the 5th Week of Easter; in my reflections, however, I shall include some of what happened at Jerusalem for it supplies background for what follows.) Perhaps as part of his technique of handling simultaneity, the author now picks up the story of the Hellenist Christians broken off in chapter 8 when he described the scattering from Jerusalem that sent them to Samaria. Belatedly we are

---

ences, e.g., as to whether the Gentiles should be required to accept some Jewish practices. Since Gentile Christians took on the coloring of the Jewish Christians who converted them, I have maintained that it is utterly useless to speak of Gentile Christianty and Jewish Christianity as if these referred to two different theological stances. In terms of relations to Judaism there was a whole range of theological stances in Jewish Christianity and a matching range in Gentile Christianity.

[59] Jewish Christians who invoked the authority of James objected to Peter's eating with Gentiles (Galatians 2:12) and thus, apparently, to his eating food that could be considered ritually unclean. Would not that objection be contrary to what Jesus had said? Mark 7:19 (alone) interprets Jesus' words to mean that he declared all foods clean. That is probably a postresurrectional insight, gained after Christians had moved in that direction. Consequently, at least from the viewpoint of chronology, Acts is plausible in having Peter discover this (through revelation) a number of years after Jesus' death.

Developments at Antioch and Jerusalem

told that they went also to Phoenicia, Cyprus, and Antioch (in Syria), preaching at first only to Jews but then gradually to Gentiles as well. This may be a tacit way of acknowledging that, although a Hebrew Christian like Peter did accept a Gentile household into the community, the really aggressive effort to convert Gentiles began with the Hellenists. When Jerusalem heard this, Barnabas was sent to Antioch to check on the development; and he approved it (11:22-23).[60] This becomes the occasion of bringing to Antioch Saul, last heard of in 9:30. Thus, while the Jerusalem church in the person of Peter is taking the first steps toward admitting a few Gentiles, Antioch develops as a second great Christian center, more vibrantly involved in mission. It is in this second center that believers in Jesus, who are now both Jews and Gentiles, receive the name "Christians" by which they will henceforth be known (11:26).

The development of the Antioch base is a grace because Jerusalem and Judea are hit particularly hard by a famine foretold by Agabus (11:27-30) and by persecution in a changed political situation where direct Roman rule had been replaced by a Jewish kingdom (12:1-23; under Herod Agrippa I: AD 41-44). The famine offers the Antiochene Christians a chance to display *koinōnia* by sharing goods with the poorer believers in Judea; the persecution offers the Jerusalem Christians an opportunity to bear witness by martyrdom, for James, son of Zebedee and brother of John, is put to death.[61] There is no move toward replacing James as there was when Judas'

[60] Nevertheless, his approval will not be enough when all the implications of the mission become apparent, and Acts 15 will tell us how at Jerusalem he and Paul had to give an account of what had happened.

[61] This is James the Greater who in legend went to Spain (venerated at Compostela) and evidently came back again to Judea soon enough to die about AD 41! He must be kept distinct from another member of the Twelve, James son of Alphaeus (about whom we know nothing), and above all from a third James, the brother of the Lord who is a dominant figure in the Jerusalem church and is not a member of the Twelve. Unfortunately the sanctoral cycle of the liturgy tends to confuse the latter two.

Chapter 4: Outreach to the Gentiles

betrayal left the sacred number of the Twelve incomplete. That is because, as I have explained, the Twelve are not to be a continuous group in history but a once-for-all-time symbol. There are only twelve thrones to judge the tribes of Israel (Luke 22:30; Matt 19:28), and it is to one of those that by his fidelity to Christ James has now gone. Acts 12:3, 11 associ-. ates the Jewish people with the antiChristian hostility of Herod, whereas hitherto in Luke-Acts there was a tendency to distinguish between the Jewish people (more favorable to Jesus) and their rulers. Readers are being prepared for a situation in which Judaism and Christianity are not only distinct but hostile.

Great danger threatens when Peter is arrested; but God intervenes through an angel to release him, even as God intervened by an angel to release him when he was arrested by the Sanhedrin (5:19). Later an earthquake will free Paul when he is in prison in Philippi (16:26). These divine interventions show God's care for the great spokesmen of the gospel.[62] That Peter, after his escape from Herod, went to another place (Acts 12:17) has given rise to the imaginative, but probably wrong, tradition that at this juncture Peter went to Rome and founded the church there. That Peter, as he left Jerusalem, sent word to James has been interpreted, also wrongly, as his passing the control of the church (and even the primacy) to James. This thesis fails to distinguish between the roles of the two men: Peter, the first of the Twelve to see the risen Jesus, is always named first among them; there is no evidence that Peter was ever local administrator of the Jerusalem church—a role of administration rejected for the Twelve in Acts 6:2. Probably as soon as there was an ad-

---

[62] In the light of such tradition, one can imagine later Christian puzzlement when neither Peter nor Paul escaped Nero's arrest at Rome where they were executed. Would some have judged that the emperor was more powerful than Christ? Perhaps that is why a book like the Apocalypse had to stress so firmly that the Lamb could and would conquer the beast representing imperial power.

Developments at Antioch and Jerusalem

ministrative role created for the Hebrew element of the Jerusalem church, James held it, not illogically because he was related to Jesus by family ties.[63] In any case Peter's departure from Jerusalem was not a permanent one; he had returned by the time of the meeting in that city described in Acts 15 (ca. AD 49). Acts finishes the colorful story of the frustrated persecution by describing (12:23) the horrible death of being eaten by worms visited by God on King Herod Agrippa in AD 44. It is quite similar to the death of the great enemy of Israel, King Antiochus Epiphanes, in II Maccabees 9:9. Both accounts are theological interpretations of sudden death: Those who dare to raise their hand against God's people face divine punishment.

The stories of famine and persecution at Jerusalem end on a triumphal note: The persecutor has fallen; God's word grows and multiplies, and Barnabas and Saul bring John Mark back with them to Antioch (12:24-25).

THE MISSION OF BARNABAS AND SAUL/PAUL FROM ANTIOCH (ACTS 13:1–14:28)

The Lectionary of the 4th and 5th Weeks of Easter shows greater interest in this section than in what has immediately preceded: two Sunday (C cycle) and six weekday readings. Here Acts begins (13:1-5) with a short description of the church of Antioch. If Jerusalem has the apostles (i.e., the Twelve), Antioch has prophets and teachers. It is scarcely accidental that Paul, whose mission would begin from Antioch, speaks of the leading charisms or gifts of the Spirit thus: "God has appointed in the church first apostles, second prophets, third teachers . . ." (I Corinthians 12:28). Acts places Barnabas and Saul among the prophets and teachers,

[63] The dominant Gospel evidence is that the "brothers" of Jesus were not disciples during his lifetime (Mark 3:31-35; 6:3-4; John 7:5); but the risen Jesus appeared to James (I Corinthians 15:7), and James was an apostle in Jerusalem at the time of Paul's conversion (Galatians 1:19; ca. AD 36).

Chapter 4: Outreach to the Gentiles

although Paul thought of himself as an apostle. Notice that Barnabas is listed first and Saul, last; only during the mission will the order be reversed to Paul and Barnabas [e.g., 13:43] and the name Paul begin to be used consistently in place of Saul. In other words in the mission the great proclaimer of the gospel will find his status and identity.

We are told that the Antiochene prophets and teachers were "performing a liturgical service [*leitourgein*] to the Lord and fasting." In Luke 5:34-35 Jesus says that the guests do not fast while the bridegroom is with them; but the days will come when the bridegroom will be taken away and then they will fast. Those days have now come and fasting has become a part of the early church life known to Luke. What did the liturgical service consist of? Was it a eucharist? Although the New Testament never gives a clear picture of any follower of Jesus presiding at the eucharist, in the light of "Do this in commemoration of me" addressed to the Twelve in the Lucan account of the Last Supper (22:19), there is no reason to doubt that members of the Twelve presided. But who presided at Antioch where the Twelve were not present? About the turn of the 1st century *Didache* 10:7 depicts a situation where prophets celebrated the eucharist, and that may have been the custom earlier as well. In this context of prayer and fasting, hands are laid on Barnabas and Saul. We should not anachronistically speak of this as an ordination; it is a commissioning by the church of Antioch for a mission that is often counted as the first of three Pauline journeys and dated to AD 46-49.

Along with John Mark, Barnabas and Saul go to Cyprus, Barnabas' home territory; and they speak in the Jewish synagogues. Since in his own writings Paul speaks of converting Gentiles, scholars have wondered whether Acts is accurate here. But the Pauline letters are to churches evangelized in later missionary journeys at a time when Paul had turned to converting Gentiles—a development that may have stemmed from experiment if he found (as Acts indicates) he was more

The Mission of Barnabas and Saul/Paul

successful with them.[64] That in fact he was involved with synagogues at some time in his missionary activity is strongly suggested by his statement in II Corinthians 11:24: "Five times I received from the Jews thirty-nine lashes." Saul's encountering in Cyprus and besting the false prophet and magus, Bar-Jesus, sets up a certain parallelism with Peter's encountering Simon Magus in Samaria. The enemies of the gospel are not simply earthly forces (as Paul will state clearly in his own letters).

Moving on from Cyprus to Asia Minor may have been a more adventurous extension of the mission than Acts indicates, and perhaps that is what caused John Mark to depart and go to Jerusalem (Acts 13:13). A later reference to this (15:37-39) shows that the behavior of John Mark left a bad memory with Paul. The author makes what happened in Asia Minor at Antioch of Pisidia almost an exemplar of the Pauline mission. Acts 13:16-41 gives a synagogue sermon of Paul (henceforth so named) that in its appeal to the Old Testament and summary of what God did in Jesus is not unlike the sermons that Acts earlier attributed to Peter.[65] Thus we get a picture of a consistent message preached by the two great figures who dominate the story of the early church, Peter and Paul. (From Paul's own words [Galatians 2:14] we know that these two men did not always agree in their appli-

[64] To the end, Acts will continue to show Paul, when he arrives at a new site, speaking first to Jews. That is dubious: Romans 1:16 indicates that in the general proclamation of the gospel Jews came first, but 11:13 characterizes Paul's own apostolate as "to the Gentiles."

[65] Undoubtedly the author of Acts composed the speech attributed to Paul; yet the composition is not alien to Pauline thought about Christ attested in his letters. For instance, Acts 13:23 relates Jesus to David's posterity and 13:33 makes God's raising Jesus the moment of saying, "You are my Son; today I have begotten you." In writing to the Romans (1:3-4) Paul speaks of the one who was "descended from David according to the flesh and designated Son of God in power according to the Spirit of holiness by resurrection from the dead." In Acts 13:39 there is justification language similar to that of the Pauline letters.

Chapter 4: Outreach to the Gentiles

cation of the gospel. Yet when it came to the essential message about Jesus, Paul associates himself with Cephas [Peter] and the Twelve [and James!] in a common preaching and a common demand for belief [I Corinthians 15:3-11].) Acts 13:42-43 reports a generally favorable reaction to the sermon, but 13:44-49 shows that on the following Sabbath there was hostility from the Jews so that Paul and Barnabas shifted their appeal to the Gentiles. The Jewish hostility continued until they were driven from Pisidia—a rebuff that evidently did not discourage them: "The disciples were filled with joy and the Holy Spirit" (13:52). Much the same thing is reported in Iconium (Acts 14:1-7).

In Lystra (14:8-11) Paul is depicted as healing a man crippled from birth just as Peter healed a cripple in 3:1-10, so that readers are now assured that the healing power of Jesus that was passed on to Peter in dealing with the Jews of Jerusalem has been passed on to Paul as well in dealing with Gentiles. The vivid Gentile reaction, hailing Barnabas and Paul as the gods Zeus and Hermes, catches the ethos of a different world where the message of the one God (14:15-18) has not really taken root, making it all the more difficult to preach Christ. (On this slender evidence, by the way, is based much speculation about the appearance of Paul as short and slight.) This time the hostility aroused by the Jews leads to the stoning of Paul and leaving him for dead. In his own writing Paul will speak eloquently about his suffering for Christ, including being stoned (e.g., II Corinthians 11:23-27); and Acts has incorporated some of that suffering in its presentation as well. In a passing phrase Acts 14:23 has Paul and Barnabas, when they revisited the cities of Asia Minor, appointing presbyters (or elders) in every church. Many doubt that this form of structure existed so early.[66] At least we may deduce from

[66] Presbyters are never mentioned in the undisputed Pauline letters; the appointment of presbyters is a major issue only in the postPauline Pastoral Epistles. Yet *episkopoi* and *diakonoi* are mentioned in Philippians 1:2, and

The Mission of Barnabas and Saul/Paul

Acts that by the last third of the 1st century when the work was written, presbyters existed in these churches and their status was seen as part of the Pauline heritage. The journey ends with a return of Paul and Barnabas to Antioch in Syria and a report to this church that had sent them forth: "God had opened a door of faith to the Gentiles" (14:26-27).

Brief Reflections on John 13-16

In a certain sense the history recounted in Acts 10-14 makes the church whole: Jews and Gentiles coming in numbers to believe in Christ. The Lectionary accompanies that story with Gospel readings from Jesus' words to "his own" (John 13:1) at the Last Supper—words set on the night before he died but clearly reaching out to believers of all times and places, telling them how to remain Jesus' own. Nowhere in the Lectionary of this season is the pattern of external happenings in Acts and internal life in John clearer.

The weekday selection of the Johannine Jesus' final words (4th Week of Easter) begins in 13:16 with the basic reminder that the servant is not greater than the master and must be willing to render the humble service that the master has just demonstrated in washing his disciples' feet. But that admonition is not accepted by the one among them who will lift up his heel against Jesus. In the light of what we have heard in Acts, this is a sober reminder that all the problems were not over when, having struggled with external opposition (Jewish and pagan), Paul and Barnabas made many converts. From the time of Jesus' death to the church today there is always danger from within, with Judas as the example of those (in or out of authority) who are not willing to remain humble disciples.

---

arguments from silence about what church structure(s) existed in Paul's lifetime are very uncertain.

Chapter 4: Outreach to the Gentiles

The main tone of the Last Discourse, however, is more encouraging, as the next Last Supper passage used by the Lectionary (John 13:31-35; 5th Sunday, C cycle) shows us. The Jesus who speaks is already glorified and will be further glorified by returning to the Father; those who keep his commandment to love one another will be truly his disciples and share in that glory. In 14:1-6 (weekday sequence) Jesus promises that there are many rooms in his Father's house where he is going to prepare the way for them. We have been reading in Acts of the lateral spread of the church on earth, but the Johannine Jesus is more interested in the vertical relation of those whom he is leaving behind on earth to his heavenly Father. If *koinōnia* with one another is a major concern of Acts, union with God is a major concern of the Last Discourse. As one who shares God's eternal life and earthly human life, Jesus is the embodiment of that union; he is the way. The disciples want to be shown the Father; yet in the long time they have been with Jesus, they have not recognized the extent to which the Father and he indwell and are one (14:8-11). If in Romans 1:13 harvesting fruit means converting people to Christ, the image of the vine and the branches in John 15 puts its emphasis on relationship to Jesus. He is the vine and one bears fruit by getting increased life from him. Disciples must participate and remain in the love that binds the Father and the Son; and as he leaves them behind, they must manifest that love as they live together. Jesus reiterates, "This I command you, to love one another" (15:17).

In the words that Jesus speaks to his own in these chapters, we encounter a major factor that influenced the church's decision to select the Johannine Last Discourse as the Gospel readings for this season. In the Introduction I pointed to the paradox that we are preparing for Pentecost, and yet the story of Acts that supplies the first readings tells us what happened *after* Pentecost and the coming of the Spirit. The paradox is partially resolved because the Last Discourse in

Brief Reflections on John 13-16

John has five passages where Jesus speaks of the coming of the Paraclete,[67] the Spirit of Truth; and the church can use them in the Lectionary of 5th and 6th Weeks of Easter to prepare for the feast of the Spirit which is now only a few days away. From the viewpoint of Christians today, Acts' story of the original Pentecost and what happened afterwards in the development of the early church is past history. However, each generation in its own life must relive the coming of the Spirit, and the Johannine Jesus' words have the power to make that possible.

In these brief reflections on John 13–16, then, let me concentrate on the unique Johannine presentation of the Paraclete, a title given to the Holy Spirit only in the Fourth Gospel. The Greek *paraklētos* means literally "one called alongside," and a standard use of the term was for one called alongside to help in a legal situation: a defense attorney. This notion is present in some of the words used to translate *paraklētos*, namely, "advocate, counsellor." There is a legal tone to some of what Jesus says about the Paraclete; yet the picture is more exactly that of a prosecuting attorney. Jesus himself is going to be crucified and die; in the eyes of the world he will be judged, found guilty, and convicted. Yet after his death, the Paraclete will come and reverse the sentence by convicting the world and proving Jesus' innocence (16:8-11). He will show that Jesus did not sin; rather the world sinned by not believing in him. He is the one who is righteousness, as is shown by the fact that he is not in the grave but with the Father. The judgment that put him to death did not defeat him; ironically it defeated his great adversary, the Prince of this world.

In a famous passage (Job 19:25) Job knows that he will go to death judged heinously guilty by all because of the sufferings visited on him; yet he knows that his vindicator lives, namely, the angel who will stand on his grave and show to

[67] 14:15-17; 14:25-26; 15:26-27; 16:7-11; 16:12-14.

Chapter 4: Outreach to the Gentiles

all that he was innocent. That vindicating angelic spirit has the role of a paraclete, and Jesus now looks for the Holy Spirit as his Paraclete. We have seen in Acts divine interventions to prove the righteousness of Peter and Paul when they were accused; and as we look for the coming of the Spirit, we look for one whose task is to be certain that ultimately injustice and evil cannot overcome those who believe.

Yet there is another role for "one called alongside": Sometimes those who suffer or are lonely need to call in someone to console and comfort them. That aspect of the Paraclete is caught by the translation "Comforter" (as in Holy Comforter), "Consoler." In the context of the Last Supper Jesus' disciples are sorrowful because he is departing; what should console them is the promise that someone just like Jesus is coming to take his place. Here we touch on a major emphasis in the Johannine presentation of the Paraclete: the likeness of the Spirit to Jesus that enables the Spirit to substitute for Jesus.[68] (That is why the Paraclete Spirit cannot come until Jesus departs.) Both come forth from the Father; both are given by the Father, or sent by the Father; both are rejected by the world. The Johannine Jesus claims to have nothing on his own; whatever he does or says is what he has heard or seen with the Father. The Paraclete will speak nothing on his own; he will take what belongs to Jesus and declare it; he will speak only what he hears (John 16:13-15). When Jesus is on earth and the Father in heaven, whoever sees Jesus sees the Father. When Jesus has gone to the Father, whoever listens to the Paraclete will be listening to Jesus. In short what Jesus is to the Father, the Paraclete is to

---

[68] Intrinsic to that notion is the idea that the Paraclete is personal. The common Greek term for "Spirit," *pneuma*, is neuter; and therefore in many New Testament passages neuter pronouns are employed: The Spirit is spoken of as "it," whether or not that is preserved in English translations. But *paraklētos* is personal (masculine), and the referential pronouns that are used are personal.

Brief Reflections on John 13-16

Jesus. Thus in many ways the Paraclete fulfills Jesus' promise to return.

In one extraordinary passage (16:7) Jesus says that it is *better* that he go away, for otherwise the Paraclete will not come. In what possible sense can the presence of the Paraclete be better than the presence of Jesus? Perhaps the solution lies in one major distinction between the presence of Jesus and that of the Paraclete. In Jesus the Word became flesh; the Paraclete is not incarnate. In the one human life of Jesus, visibly, at a definite time and a definite place, God's presence was uniquely in the world; and then corporally Jesus left this world and went to the Father. The Paraclete's presence is not visible, not confined to any one time or place. Rather the Paraclete dwells in everyone who loves Jesus and keeps the commandments, and so his presence is not limited by time (14:15-17). That may be the way in which the coming of the Paraclete is "better." These words of Jesus about the Paraclete illustrate beautifully how the audience to which he speaks at the Last Supper extends beyond those present at that moment. In terms of the presence of God as the Paraclete there are no second-class citizens: The Paraclete is just as present in the modern disciples of Jesus as he was in the first generation.

That fact is particularly important when we consider one of the principal activities of the Paraclete. The Paraclete is the Spirit of Truth who supplies guidance along the way of all truth. The Johannine Jesus had many things to say that his disciples could never understand in his lifetime (16:12); but then the Paraclete comes and takes those things and declares them (16:15). In other words the Paraclete solves the problem of new insights into a past revelation. When God gave the Son, divine revelation was granted in all its completeness: Jesus was the very Word of God. Yet that Word spoke audibly under the limitations of a particular culture and set of issues. How do Christians of other ages get God's guidance for dealing with entirely different issues in a very different

Chapter 4: Outreach to the Gentiles

culture? Jesus' words make clear that the Paraclete who is present to every time and culture brings no new revelation; rather he takes the revelation of the Word made flesh and declares it anew, facing the things to come. We see from the words of Paul to the presbyters of Ephesus in Acts 20:28-31 that one reason for the establishment of the presbyteral church structure was to protect the faithful from strange perversions of truth. The Pauline Pastoral Epistles also envision presbyter-bishops who hold on to the doctrine they have received as a criterion for judging what is valid in any new approaches. Thus at a time when other churches were developing such an external teaching magisterium to guide all those under pastoral care, John places the emphasis on the indwelling Paraclete, the guide to all truth, given to every believer. There has been a tendency in Christian history to allow one or the other of these approaches to dominate; but as the sole approach each one has drawbacks. Teachers whose only strength is to hold on to the tradition may tend to regard all new ideas as dangerous. The Spirit is a vibrant guide and would seem better adapted to face the things to come; yet when two believers who claim the guidance of the indwelling Paraclete disagree, often neither can see a way in which he or she can be wrong, and the tendency is to split into irreconcilable divisions. By reading John alongside Acts, implicitly the church is reminding itself that guidance for Christians involves an interplay between external instruction by well-grounded teachers and internal movements of the Paraclete. Both factors are essential to enable the church to combine valid tradition and new insights without breaking the *koinōnia*.

The Jesus of the Last Supper who prepares his disciples for the coming of the Spirit is not unrealistic. The world will hate the disciples who have received the Spirit of Truth (15:18-19) which the world cannot accept because it neither sees nor recognizes that Spirit (14:17). The disciples will be expelled from the synagogues and even put to death (16:2-3),

Brief Reflections on John 13-16

a Johannine parallel to some of the treatment of Paul that Acts narrates. Yet because Jesus is with them, they can have peace. "In the world you will have trouble; but take courage, I have overcome the world" (16:33).

Chapter 4: Outreach to the Gentiles

Chapter 5

The Jerusalem Conference Propels the Church to the Ends of the Earth (Acts 15-28)

If what Paul had done pleased the church at Antioch, it did not please the circumcision party at Jerusalem who now send people to Antioch to challenge the acceptance of Gentiles without circumcision. One might have thought that this issue was settled at Jerusalem earlier (Acts 11) when Peter justified his acceptance of the Gentile Cornelius without circumcision. It was, however, one thing to incorporate into a largely Jewish Christian community a few Gentiles; it was another to be faced with whole churches of Gentiles such as Paul had founded—churches that would have little relation to Judaism other than holding in veneration the Jewish Scriptures.

We can see in Romans 11:13-36 Paul's understanding of what he thought would happen from his Gentile mission: The Gentiles were a wild olive branch grafted on the tree of Israel; and eventually, through envy, all Israel would come to faith in Christ and be saved.

The circumcision party may have been far more realistic in their fears that Paul had begun a process whereby Christianity would become an almost entirely Gentile religion, which of course is what happened. (Ultraconservatives, as distorted as their theology may be, are often more perceptive about the inevitable direction of changes than are the moderates who propose them.) Far from being grafted on the tree of Israel, the Gentile Christians became the tree. To stop that foreseeable catastrophe Paul's opponents attack the principle that Gentiles may be admitted without becoming Jews (i.e., being circumcised). They cause enough trouble that Paul and Barnabas have to go to Jerusalem to debate the issue. What follows is a report of what may be judged the most important meeting or conference[69] ever held in the history of Christianity, for it decided the question of whether Christianity would be a minor Jewish sect or would soon become a separate religion reaching to the ends of the earth.

Selections from this chapter of Acts are read on the 6th Sunday of Easter (C year) and on three days of the Fifth Week.

We are fortunate in having two accounts of the Jerusalem conference, one in Acts 15, the other in Galatians 2; and this double perspective teaches us much about the great personalities of early Christianity. Scholars tend to prefer Paul's own account as an eyewitness and to regard the Acts account as later bowdlerizing. There is no question that Acts presents a simplified and less acrimonious report; but as regards Galatians, we should recognize that a personal account written in self-defense has its own optic that removes it from the realm of the purely objective. For instance, in Galatians 2:1 Paul says, "I went up to Jerusalem with Barnabas, taking Titus along with me"; Acts 15:2 says that "Paul and Barnabas and some others were appointed to go up to Jerusalem." That they went up commissioned by the church of Antioch may very well be the more accurate picture, even though (as part of his self-defense in Galatians) Paul highlights his initiative in cooperating. It is very clear from Acts that those in Jerusalem had the power of decision on the issue. Paul speaks disparagingly of the "so-called pillars" whose reputation meant nothing to him; but, of course, that title implies that their reputation did mean something to others, and in the long run Paul could not stand alone. True, as he claims, he got his gospel (of the freely given grace to the Gentiles)

---

[69] Very often this is called the Council of Jerusalem, but preferably the term "council" is avoided because people tend to confuse it with later ecumenical councils of the church (Nicaea, etc.).

Chapter 5: The Jerusalem Conference and Aftermath

through a revelation from Jesus Christ and would not change it even if an angel told him to do so (Galatians 1:8, 11-12); yet he mentions the possibility that he had run in vain (2:2). If that is more than an oratorical touch, he may have been admitting the power of the "pillars": Should they deny his Gentile churches *koinōnia* with the mother church in Jerusalem, there would be a division that negated the very nature of the church. Thus, despite Paul's certitude about the rightness of his evangelizing, the outcome of the Jerusalem meeting for the communities he had evangelized involved uncertainty.

To have brought along Titus, an uncircumcised Gentile (Galatians 2:3), was a shrewd maneuver. Probably some of the circumcision party[70] had never seen any of the uncircumcised Gentiles whom they denied to be true Christians; and it is always more difficult to confront others who patently believe in Christ and tell them face to face, "You are not Christians because you do not agree with me." Another prudent step by Paul (Galatians 2:2) was first to lay out his argument privately before those at Jerusalem who were of repute. First reactions of authorities are often defensive; when they are uttered in private, they can be modified later without loss of face. Some tragedies could have been averted in the post-Vatican II Catholic Church if those eager for change had stayed away from the front page of newspapers. Such "eyeball-to-eyeball" confrontations with authorities usually proved little more than nearsightedness.

The public disputation, however, is the core of the story. Four participants were involved, two predictable and two unpredictable. Predictable were the unnamed spokesmen of the circumcision party who demanded that the Gentiles be circumcised in order to become fully Christian and, on the

[70] In place of this more neutral terminology of Acts (which in 15:5 also specifies that they were members of the party of the Pharisees), Paul speaks polemically of "false brethren" spying out the freedom of his treatment of the Gentiles.

The Great Crisis Settled by the Jerusalem Conference

other extreme, Paul and his companions who argued that to demand circumcision would nullify the dispensation of grace by Christ. Unpredictable were Peter, who as the first of the Twelve had a responsibility toward the whole people of the renewed Israel, and James, who with the elders represented the leadership of the Hebrew Christian community of Jerusalem. Arguments from three of the four participants are reported. Understandably, given the goal of Galatians, Paul's account is centered on his own role, not yielding submission even for a moment and convincing the reputed pillars of the truth of his gospel. Yet Acts gives the least space to Barnabas and Paul (15:12), sandwiching their report between Peter's words (15:6-11) and those of James (15:13-21)—an arrangement creating the impression that it is the last who carried the day. Probably one needs to read between the lines of both accounts. The issue to be discussed was what Paul and Barnabas had done in their missionary activity, and in that sense the conference was centered on Paul. Yet his reasoning was probably implicit in what he had done and was not likely to persuade those still undecided; therefore Acts may very well be correct in the proportion it gives to Paul's remarks. Peter's stance favorable to Gentiles was already known at Jerusalem, and so the real suspense may have been centered on what James would say, since he would carry the Jerusalem church with him. Galatians 2:9 recognizes that by listing James ahead of Cephas (Peter) and John as the so-called pillars of the church.

What was the reasoning advanced? Acts says that Barnabas and Paul recounted the signs and wonders done among the Gentiles; Galatians says that Paul related to them the gospel he preached among the Gentiles, which surely meant an account of how such people had come to faith without circumcision. If Galatians 1 is a guide, Paul's self-understanding was that, if God had freely called him while he was persecuting Christians, God's grace was given freely without previous demands. According to Acts Peter's argument was

Chapter 5: The Jerusalem Conference and Aftermath

also experiential: Gentiles had to be accepted without distinctions and imposed burdens because God had sent the Holy Spirit on the uncircumcised Cornelius. James' argument in Acts is reasoned and, as might be expected from a conservative Hebrew Christian, draws upon the Law. The prophets foretold that the Gentiles would come, and the Law of Moses allowed uncircumcised Gentiles to live among the people of God provided that they abstained from certain listed pollutions. Unfortunately we do not hear the arguments advanced by the circumcision party, other than the simple statement in Acts 15:5 that the Law of Moses required circumcision.

What is startling is a deafening silence. No one who favors admitting the Gentiles without circumcision mentions the example of Jesus, saying, "Jesus told us to do so." And, of course, the reason is that he never did tell them to do so. Indeed, one may suspect that the only ones likely to have mentioned Jesus would have been those of the circumcision party, arguing precisely that there was no authorization from him for such a radical departure from the Law.[71] This may have been the first of many times when those who have resisted change in the church did so by arguing that Jesus never did this, whereas those who promoted change did so on the import of Christ for a situation that the historical Jesus did not encounter. In any case, both Acts and Galatians agree that Peter (and John) and James kept the *koinōnia* with Paul and his Gentile churches. The road was now open for free and effective evangelizing to the ends of the earth. In fact that road would also lead away from Judaism. Whatever nonChristian Jews thought of Christian Jews, they were

---

[71] The Synoptic Gospels give attention to Jesus' reaching out to tax-collectors and prostitutes. Was part of the reason for preserving that memory an implicit rebuttal of the circumcision position? One could construct the rebuttal thus: Jesus did reach out to those outside the Law, and now in our time the Gentiles are the ones outside the Law. One must recognize, however, that such arguments offer their own difficulties, for they can be used to justify almost any practice.

The Great Crisis Settled by the Jerusalem Conference

bound together by having been born into the chosen people. There would be no such ties to Christian Gentiles; and even though the Savior for those Gentiles was a Jew born under the Law, Christianity would soon be looked on as a Gentile religion quite alien to a Judaism for which the Law would become ever more important once the Temple was destroyed.

THE RETURN TO ANTIOCH; WIDER PAULINE
MISSIONARY ACTIVITY (ACTS 15:30–21:14)
Reasonably consecutive readings from Acts 16-20 constitute the selections in the Lectionary for ten weekdays from the end of the 5th Week of Easter into the middle of the 7th Week.

Acts 15:30-39: The Return to Antioch. According to Acts Paul and Barnabas went back to Antioch with Judas and Silas, carrying a letter that made it clear that circumcision was not to be required of Gentile converts. However, the Gentiles were to be required to abstain from four things proscribed by Leviticus 17-18 for aliens living among Israel: meat offered to idols; the eating of blood; the eating of strangled animals (i.e., animals that were not ritually slaughtered); and incestuous unions (*porneia,* "impurity," but here with kin). This is the position that James advocated when he spoke at the Jerusalem conference. When we compare the picture to Paul's account in Galatians 2:11ff., we realize that the history was probably more complicated. A plausible combination of the two sources of information yields something like the following. Paul and Barnabas went back to Antioch with the good news that freedom from circumcision had been recognized. However, struggles developed as to whether Gentile Christians were bound by food laws as were the Jewish Christians who constituted the church alongside them. Paul argued that they were not bound, and Peter participated in this free practice until men from James came demanding spe-

Chapter 5: The Jerusalem Conference and Aftermath

cific practices of the food laws.[72] Peter acceded to James, much to Paul's anger. Probably so also did Barnabas and John Mark; for Acts, which is silent about the struggle between Paul and Peter, reports a quarrel between Paul and those other two figures, so that they would no longer travel together (15:36-40). When Paul set out on another mission, it was Silas he took. In the churches he would convert (where Gentile Christians would have been the majority) the Gentiles were not bound by Jewish food laws, as we see from Paul's letters. Apparently in the area where James of Jerusalem had influence (Acts 15:23: Antioch, Syria, and Cilicia, where presumably Jewish Christians were the majority), the Gentiles were bound. Through the Jerusalem conference the *koinōnia* had been preserved as to what was essential for conversion: Gentiles did not have to become Jews. However, this did not guarantee uniformity of lifestyle. Paul thought that freedom from the food laws was so important that it was an issue of gospel truth (Galatians 2:14); apparently others did not think it that important. We can learn a lesson today from this later struggle: Too often there has been an insistence on uniformity. Only with great care should comparable differences, no matter how deeply felt, become a litmus test of true Christianity or true Catholicism.

Acts 15:40-21:14: Wider Pauline Missionary Activity. It is customary to detect in Acts three Pauline missionary journeys, with one journey (AD 46-49) before the Jerusalem conference and two after it (AD 50-52, 54-58). We are uncertain, however, that the author of Acts made such a division, for it is easy to look on everything from 15:40 to 21:14 as one long journey.[73] What is certain is that, after the Jerusalem decision, Acts

[72] Galatians 2:12. Scholars are divided on whether the men from James included Judas and Silas bringing the letter mentioned in Acts.

[73] Only one extemely brief passage (18:22-24) would encourage us to divide it. In any case, the division into journeys is entirely based on Acts, not on Paul's own expressed memories, even though he could supply a chronological calculation of his visits to Jerusalem (Galatians 2:1).

The Return to Antioch

describes Paul's major missionary activity as ranging much
farther than his first missionary effort. It is now that, after
retracing his previous journey, he went to northern Galatia,
and crossed over to Greece (Philippi, Thessalonica, Athens,
Corinth), coming back to Ephesus in Asia Minor and finally
back to Antioch. Then setting out once more from Antioch
he went to Ephesus for two years and from there he wrote to
some of the churches just mentioned (probably Galatians,
Philippians, and part of the Corinthian correspondence). Subsequent travels brought him to Macedonia and Corinth,
travels that offered an occasion for the writing of the rest of
the Corinthian correspondence and the letter to the Romans.
It is almost as if the Jerusalem decision made possible the
most creative time of Paul's life.

The narrative begins with the circumcision of Timothy in
Acts 16:1-5, the reliability of which action is questioned by
many scholars. They think it inconceivable that Paul would
have changed his stance on circumcision even to win converts. However, if Timothy was looked on as a Jew, we have
no clear evidence that Paul would have wanted Jewish Christians to give up circumcision. The words in Galatians 5:2, "If
you receive circumcision, Christ will be of no advantage to
you," are addressed to Gentiles. Romans 9:4-5 speaks of the
privileges of Paul's "kinsmen according to the flesh," the
Israelites: To them belong the sonship, the glory, the
covenants, the giving of the Law, the worship, the promises,
the patriarchs. Why deprive Timothy of this birthright? At
least some Christians must have thought that way, and this
disputable issue is indicative of how complex it must have
been to be a Jew who believed in Jesus.

Paul's vision of the man of Macedonia in 16:9-10 that
causes him to cross over to Greece is seen by the author of
Acts as a divinely inspired moment. The spread of Christian
faith to Europe is presented almost as manifest destiny; and
in retrospect the tremendous contributions of two thousand
years of European Christianity would justify that judgment.

Chapter 5: The Jerusalem Conference and Aftermath

Far more than the author of Acts could have dreamed, the appeal of the man of Macedonia ultimately brought Christianity to ends of the earth that in the 1st century were not even known to exist. Some on other continents who were evangelized from Europe complain that they were indoctrinated with an alien culture. Yet Europeanization would probably have happened in any case; and the fact that the cross of Christ was planted alongside the banner of the respective king was potentially a helpful corrective—both to abuses that existed before Europeans came (that are sometimes forgotten) and to the abuses they brought.

The evangelizing at Philippi (16:11-40) shows us some of the best and the worst of a mission among Gentiles. The generous openness and support of Lydia, a Gentile devotee of Jewish worship, is a model for the Christian household. On the other hand, the legal and financial problems presented by the girl who had a spirit of divination remind us that Paul was dealing with an alien, superstitious world. As the account continues, the miraculous opening of the prison echoes scenes of Peter's miraculous release from prison and shows that God is with his emissary to the Gentiles. The complexity of Paul's trial because he is a Roman citizen illustrates how the early Christians, in order to survive, had to use every available means, including Roman law.

At Thessalonica (17:1-9) Paul runs into the same kind of Jewish opposition that marred his mission in Asia Minor before the Jerusalem conference. The list of charges against Paul and his supporters in 17:6-7 resembles the list of charges against Jesus before Pilate in Luke 23:2—a list found only in Luke.[74] Before we finish, we shall see other resemblances between the treatment of Jesus and the treatment of Paul, undoubtedly a parallelism that fitted the theology of Luke-Acts.

---

[74] The more formal character of the Roman trial of Jesus in Luke probably stems from the familiarity of the author with Roman procedures against individual Christians in his own time.

Wider Pauline Mission

Jewish opposition forces Paul to go on to Beroea where in an interesting gesture of evenhandedness the author tells us that the Jews were nobler and less contentious. But the Jews from Thessalonica follow, and so Paul pushes on to Athens (17:15).

Just as the author of Acts exhibited a sense of destiny when Paul crossed to Europe, he shows an appreciation of what Athens meant to Greek culture in recounting Paul's stay there. He supplies a dramatic context of Epicurean and Stoic philosophers (17:18) who try to fit this new teaching into their categories. The author knows about the agora or public square (17:17) and the hill of the Areopagus (17:19); and the sermon delivered there by Paul draws on an awareness of the many temples and statues of the city. The play on the altar to an unknown god and the philosophical and poetic quotations offer a cultured approach to the message about Christ, quite unlike the gambits of the other sermons in Acts. The master-touch in the scene may be the reaction to this eloquence from the cosmopolitan audience: Some mock; others put Paul off; some believe. Paul will go from here directly to Corinth, and in I Corinthians 2:1-2 he describes what may have been a lesson learned: "When I came to you proclaiming the mystery of God, I did not come with lofty words or wisdom. For I decided to know nothing among you except Jesus Christ and him crucified."

By comparing Athens to other great cities in the Roman Empire of the 1st century one can evaluate strengths and priorities in the Christian mission. Athens was the center of culture, philosophy, and art; Paul's message had only limited success there, and we are told of no other early mission to the city. Alexandria was the center of learning with its magnificent library tradition; the eloquent preacher Apollos came from there (Acts 18:24), but otherwise (and despite later legends) we know of no pre-70 Christian missionary activity there. Rome was the seat of imperial power and ruled the world. There was a successful Christian mission in the capital by the 40s; Paul could address plural house churches there

Chapter 5: The Jerusalem Conference and Aftermath

before 60; various New Testament writings are thought to have been addressed to or sent by the church of Rome; and ultimately Peter and Paul would die there. Why greater attention to Rome than to Athens or Alexandria? An answer detectable beneath the symbolism may be that Christians were realists; neither Athens the museum nor Alexandria the library could sway the world, and so the powerful city that did was a better target.

Paul's stay at Corinth (18:1-18) has an added interest because of the later correspondence that he would direct to that church (causing us to know more about it than about any other Pauline church) and because characters like Aquila and Priscilla (Prisca) will feature in that correspondence. These two figures who had come from Rome (probably already as Christians) will eventually go back to Rome and be part of Paul's contacts ("co-workers in Christ Jesus") with that city before he ever gets there (Romans 16:3). Since we have already heard of Silas and Timothy, we can see Paul forming a circle of colleagues and friends who would be in contact with him all his life. Just as the disciples of Jesus carried on the master's work, the co-workers of Paul would continue the apostle's work and literature in the postPauline period. The reference to tent-making at the beginning of Paul's stay at Corinth reminds us of the indication in his letters that he normally supported himself and did not ask his hearers for personal financial help (also Acts 20:33-35). Once again we see Jewish hostility so that Paul is brought before the tribunal of the Roman proconsul Gallio—a figure whose presence at Corinth supplies a most important key for dating Paul's mission there to AD 51–52. The unwillingness of the Roman official to get involved in Jewish religious questions is part of the general picture given of the pre-Nero period when Rome was not yet hostile to Christians as such. The tribunal or *bēma* of Corinth has recently been excavated and may be seen in the agora or market, a reminder of how Christianity was now being proclaimed in places and before people verifiably historical.

Wider Pauline Mission

Once Paul leaves Corinth, Acts crowds into a few verses (that may even be confused) a return through Ephesus and Caesarea to Jerusalem (18:22a?) and back to Ephesus. The Lectionary skips even that brief report and follows Acts 18:24–19:40 in concentrating on scenes in Ephesus, another great center of Pauline activity (more than two years) and of future importance for the church. Here the author tells us of Apollos from Alexandria and others who believed in Jesus but had received only the baptism of John and knew nothing of the Holy Spirit. Little enlightenment is given about how such a situation could exist—were these evangelized by some who knew Jesus during the ministry but left Palestine before the crucifixion and resurrection? Acts has told us before and tells us again of Paul's struggles with synagogue Jews and with devotees of pagan deities, divination, and magic; but this is one of the few times that it hints at a confrontation with competing Christian preachers, a struggle that has a major place in much of the Pauline correspondence.

Alas, such conflicts offer us background for our church situation today where Christians are struggling not only with a secular world that looks on faith in Christ as an antiquated superstition but also with each other over different presentations of the gospel. Acts 19:11-17 piques our interest with a portrait of Paul the miracle-worker and of Jewish exorcists attempting to drive out evil spirits using the name of Jesus—another reminder of how closely the ministry of the early church resembled the ministry of Jesus. Several times previously in Acts when describing the success of the ministry, the author stopped to report that the word of God increased or grew (6:7; 12:24), and now he repeats that refrain (19:20). It signals that alongside Jerusalem and Antioch, Christianity has now another great center, Ephesus, and that Paul's ministry has been blessed even as was the ministry of the Twelve.

Acts 19:21 is the first indication of Paul's ultimate plan to go to Rome via Greece and Jerusalem, an important anticipa-

Chapter 5: The Jerusalem Conference and Aftermath

tion for how the book will end. The Lectionary skips over the colorful account of the silversmiths' riot centered on Artemis or Diana of the Ephesians (19:23-40) as well as the travels through Macedonia to Troas where Paul raised the dead to life (20:1-12). It would be of interest to know if Paul's breaking bread in 20:11 means that he presided at the eucharist. What does appear in full in the Lectionary is the eloquent farewell sermon given at Miletus to the presbyters of the church of Ephesus (20:17-38). Earlier I mentioned the problem of whether Acts' account of Paul appointing presbyters on his first missionary journey was anachronistic, and that same issue has been raised here. Nevertheless this sermon has great value as a guide to how the author of Acts sees the presbyters inheriting the care of the church from Paul. In the Pastoral Epistles there is information suggesting that, after going to Rome and being released from prison, Paul came back to Asia Minor in the mid 60s. Acts betrays no knowledge of this, so that the sermon constitutes Paul's final directives to those whom he will never see again (20:25, 38).[75] It begins with an *apologia pro vita sua* (20:18-21) as Paul reflects on how he has served the Lord; this yields to foreboding about the imprisonment and afflictions he must now undergo. This man who first encountered the profession of Christ in Jerusalem some twenty years before at the trial and stoning of Stephen is being led by the Spirit to return to that city where he will be put on trial amidst cries for his death (see 22:22). In this portentous context Paul admonishes the presbyters he is leaving behind to be shepherds of the flock in which the Holy Spirit has made them overseers (20:28: *episkopos*).[76]

[75] This portion of Acts resembles the context of the Pastoral Epistles where the time of Paul's departure has come (II Timothy 4:6-8). In fact both Acts and the Pastorals (in that order) were most likely written after Paul's death. Many scholars think that of the existing correspondence Romans was the last letter actually written by Paul and contains his last preserved thoughts.

[76] *Episkopos*, literally "one who oversees," is the Greek word for bishop.

Wider Pauline Mission

As we can see from I Peter 5:1-4, the comparison of the presbyters to shepherds of the flock was well established in the late 1st century. Although that image contains within it a note of authority, the real emphasis is on the obligation to take care of the flock and not let it be ravaged—in short, what we mean by "*pastoral* care," a terminology derived from shepherding. The most pressing danger, as also in the Pastoral Epistles, is false teaching: "those who speak perverse things so as to draw away disciples" (Acts 20:30). Subsequently churches with strong doctrinal emphasis have found in such a passage the roots of a teaching magisterium that is vigilant against error. In this context Paul stresses that he supported himself, coveting no one's silver and gold (20:33-35), and indeed elsewhere in the New Testament advice to presbyters warns against a corrupting love of money (I Peter 5:2; Titus 1:7; I Timothy 3:3), an enduring temptation since the presbyters managed the common funds. After this farewell at Miletus, Acts (21:1-14) tells us more briefly of other dramatic farewells at Tyre and Caesarea, with the supernatural warnings of impending doom growing more intense.

ARREST AT JERUSALEM; IMPRISONMENT;
SENT TO ROME FOR JUDGMENT (ACTS 21:15-28:31)
Clearly then it is with a sense of approaching climax that we read finally that Paul went up to Jerusalem. His report of success among the Gentiles (presumably accompanied by the collection of money for the Christian poor of Judea of which we learn from the letters) is welcomed by James and the elders who match his claims with reports of their own successes among the Jews. Even Acts, which unlike Paul's letters has not signaled his expectation of a less than enthusiastic reception by the Jerusalem Christian authorities,

---

Once more we are close to the atmosphere of the Pastorals where there are groups of presbyter-bishops in the postPauline churches, i.e., presbyters who oversee the community's life and teaching.

Chapter 5: The Jerusalem Conference and Aftermath

cannot disguise the negative feelings raised by rumors about what Paul has been teaching.[77] (Evidently the nasty habit of misjudging one's fellow Christians based on hear-say without personally verifying the facts goes back to Christian beginnings.)

The well-intentioned plan to have Paul show his loyalty to Judaism by purifying himself and going to the Temple (21:24) fails when fanatics start a riot claiming that he has defiled the holy place by bringing Gentiles into it. Paul is saved from the crowd only by the intervention of a Roman tribune with soldiers who arrest him. The Lectionary ignores all this as well as Paul's speech of defense (22:3-21) in which he recounts his conversion. After the readings from Paul's speech to the Ephesian elders at Miletus in Acts 20, the Lectionary picks up Paul's story with 22:30; 23:6-11 when he stands before the Sanhedrin and arouses dissent between the Sadducees and Pharisees over the resurrection. There are echoes here of Jesus' dealing with the Sadducees over the resurrection (Luke 20:27) and his appearance before the Sanhedrin. The fate of Paul the great disciple is not different from the fate of his master. The parallelism is heightened by the next Lectionary selection as it races to end the readings from Acts in the last week of Easter. From the many-chaptered account of Paul's trials and imprisonment, it chooses 25:13-21 where the Roman governor Festus who has inherited Paul as a prisoner brings him before the Herodian king Agrippa II to be heard, even as in Luke's passion (23:6-12) Pilate turned Jesus over to Herod Antipas. Neither Herodian king finds the prisoner guilty.

The last reading in the prePentecost Lectionary is appropriately from the last chapter in Acts (28:16-20, 30-31) as Paul

---

[77] We can deduce from Paul's letters that he never taught the Gentiles to follow admonitions such as those found in the apostolic letter of Acts 15:23-29, restricting their freedom, a letter James reminds him of in 21:25. However, we have no evidence that he taught "all the Jews who live among the Gentiles to forsake Moses" (21:21).

Arrest at Jerusalem

comes to Rome after his long and treacherous sea journey. Unfortunately it does not contain the magnificent understatement in 28:14, "And so we came to Rome." This is the ultimate step foreseen by the risen Jesus: "You shall be my witnesses in Jerusalem and Judea and Samaria and *to the ends of the earth*." By the time Paul came to the capital in the early 60s, Christian communities had been there for about twenty years. But in the flow of the story that has centered on Peter and Paul, the climax comes with the arrival in Rome of the great missionary. The irony is that Roman authorities have sent him there because of his appeal to the emperor, and thus have been responsible for the evangelizing of their own empire. To the very end of its account Acts portrays Paul appealing to the local Jews with the insistence that he has done nothing "against the customs of our fathers."[78] Nevertheless his preaching to them about Jesus has no success, and the last words attributed to him in the book despair of ever getting a hearing from Jews and a firm decision to turn to the Gentiles who will listen. Clearly the author expects the Christian message to be carried out to the whole empire. The summary that ends the book speaks of Paul's preaching two years in Rome with success.

Brief Reflections on John 17 and John 21

In the last week of the prePentecost season the Lectionary employs as Gospel readings the Johannine Jesus' "high priestly" prayer in John 17 and his last words to Simon Peter

[78] Acts 28:21 is important: The author portrays the Jewish community in Jerusalem as being in close contact with the Jewish community in Rome (which may well be factual). That the Jews in Rome have heard nothing hostile about Paul is odd, since in writing to the Romans Paul seems to expect hostility upon arrival from Christians who are particularly attached to Judaism. I have discussed this in *Antioch and Rome* (New York: Paulist, 1982), 111–22.

Chapter 5: The Jerusalem Conference and Aftermath

and the beloved disciple in John 21. The prayer constitutes one of the most exalted pages in the New Testament as the Johannine Jesus speaks to the Father of the completion of the work assigned him. That work, as we have seen, involved the gift of eternal life, a life centered on the intimate knowledge of the one true God and of Jesus who was sent. Those whom the Father has given Jesus have been entrusted with such revealed knowledge, and Jesus prays for them. His assertion "I do not pray for the world" (17:9) startles us today, especially after Vatican Council II which took a generally positive attitude toward the possibilities offered by the modern world. Yet the distinction Jesus makes about being in the world but not of it (17:14-15) is valid. Although God manifested love for the world in sending the only Son (3:16), by the end of the Gospel the world represents those who have preferred darkness to light. Jesus' own are not part of that world which has a Prince of its own, the evil one. The only one of Jesus' companions who belongs to the world is Judas, the son of destruction (17:12), the one into whom Satan entered (13:2, 27). The rest are protected by the name that the Father has given to Jesus (17:11-12)[79] and that he has revealed to them (17:6, 26).

Throughout the Last Discourse Jesus has been speaking through and beyond his disciples to believers of all time. The prayer makes that explicit in 17:20: "It is not for these alone that I pray but also for those who believe in me through their word." The special focus of this prayer for subsequent believers is "that they all may be one," as Jesus returns to the attitude of the Good Shepherd (10:16). The story we have

[79] We saw that baptism in the name of Jesus probably meant confessing the name by which Jesus' status was acknowledged (Lord, Messiah [Christ], Savior, Son of God, etc.). Sometimes that confession is connected to what happened at the resurrection/exaltation, e.g., "God greatly exalted him and bestowed on him the name that is above every other name . . . Jesus Christ is Lord" (Philippians 2:9-11). John is clear that Jesus possessed the name (Son of Man? I AM?) during his earthly life.

Brief Reflections on John 17 and John 21

heard in the readings from Acts stressed *koinōnia* in the face
of divisions among Christians; and now John 17:22-23 gives a
most realistic reason for Jesus' disciples being one, namely,
that "the world may know that you sent me." One of the
greatest obstacles to evangelizing others about Jesus is a lack
of love among Christians, and so Jesus prays that the love
the Father had for him before the creation of the world "may
be in them and I may be in them" (17:24, 26).

After the prayer the Lectionary turns to John 21:15-25.
Roughly at the same Lectionary moment when Paul in Acts
is speaking his last words to the presbyters whom he has appointed in the church of Ephesus, instructing them to keep
watch over the flock, Jesus speaks his last words to Simon
Peter instructing him to feed the lambs. As I have stressed
above, this belated introduction of human pastoral care into
the Johannine picture manages to keep alive the ideal of the
one good shepherd. The sheep still belong to Jesus, and
Simon Peter must show his care for them by the way he
dies. It is ironical that having received his pastoral assign-
ment Peter's first reaction is typical of many in church structure ever since: He is worried about the beloved disciple who
seems to be a threat because he does not fit in. Jesus' corrective is sharp and perceptively enduring: "How does that concern you? Your concern is to follow me." Although Peter is
given pastoral authority, it is of the beloved disciple who
holds no position in church structure that Jesus says, "Sup-
pose I would like him to remain until I come"—a consoling
thought for the vast majority whose only position in the
church is to be disciples. A discipleship of love is what really
matters in the eyes of the Johannine Jesus, and that will en-
dure. No wonder that the evangelist's last words (21:25)
about such a Jesus (and the Lectionary's last words in the
prePentecostal season) are that all the books in the world
cannot do him justice.

Chapter 5: The Jerusalem Conference and Aftermath

LECTIONARY READINGS
(FIRST AND THIRD)
FOR THE SUNDAY MASSES
AFTER EASTER UNTIL PENTECOST

2d Sunday of Easter (Low Sunday)

ACTS

A. 2:42-47
B. 4:32-35
C. 5:12-16

Appearances
of the
Risen Jesus

3d Sunday of Easter

A. 2:14, 22-28
B. 3:13-15, 17-19
C. 5:27-32, 40-41

taken from
Luke and
John

4th Sunday of Easter

JOHN

A. 2:14, 36-41
B. 4:8-12
C. 13:14, 43-52

10:1-10
10:11-18
10:27-30

5th Sunday of Easter

A. 6:1-7
B. 9:26-31
C. 14:21-27

14:1-12
15:1-8
13:31-33a, 34-35

6th Sunday of Easter

A. 8:5-8, 14-17
B. 10:25-26, 34-35, 44-48
C. 15:1-2, 22-29

14:15-21
15:19-27
14:23-29

7th Sunday of Easter

A. 1:12-14
B. 1:15-17, 20-26
C. 7:55-60

John 17:1-11
17:11-19
17:20-26

Pentecost Sunday

2:1-11

20:19-23

Liturgical Readings Between Easter and Pentecost

LECTIONARY READINGS
FOR THE WEEKDAY MASSES
AFTER EASTER UNTIL PENTECOST

1st (Octave) Week of Easter

ACTS

2:14, 22-32	Appearances
2:36-41	of the
3:1-10	Risen Jesus
3:11-26	taken from
4:1-12	the
4:13-21	Four Gospels

2d Week of Easter

JOHN

4:23-31	John 3:1-8
4:32-37	3:7-15
5:17-26	3:16-21
5:27-33	3:31-36
5:34-42	6:1-15
6:1-7	6:16-21

3d Week of Easter

6:8-15	6:22-29
7:51–8:1a	6:30-35
8:1b-8	6:35-40
8:26-40	6:44-51
9:1-20	6:52-59
9:31-42	6:60-69

Liturgical Readings Between Easter and Pentecost

4th Week of Easter

11:1-18	10:1-10 (or 10:11-18 in A year)
11:19-26	10:22-30
12:24–13:5	12:44-50
13:13-25	13:16-20
13:26-33	14:1-6
13:44-52	14:7-14

5th Week of Easter

14:5-18	14:21-26
14:19-28	14:27-31
15:1-6	15:1-8
15:7-21	15:9-11
15:22-31	15:12-17
16:1-10	15:18-21

6th Week of Easter

16:11-15	15:26–16:4
16:22-34	16:5-11
17:15-22; 18:1	16:12-15
18:1-8 (when not the Feast of the Ascension)	16:16-20
18:9-18	16:20-23a
18:23-28	16:23b-28

7th Week of Easter

19:1-8	16:29-33
20:17-27	17:1-11a
20:28-38	17:11b-19
22:30; 23:6-11	17:20-26
25:13-21	21:15-19
28:16-20, 30-31	21:20-25

Liturgical Readings Between Easter and Pentecost

Works of Raymond E. Brown published by The Liturgical Press:

A Coming Christ in Advent (Matthew 1 and Luke 1)
An Adult Christ at Christmas (Matthew 2 and Luke 2)
A Crucified Christ in Holy Week (Passion Narratives)
A Risen Christ in Eastertime (Resurrection Narratives)
A Once-and-Coming Spirit at Pentecost (Acts and John)

The Gospels and Epistles of John—A Concise Commentary
Recent Discoveries and the Biblical World (A Michael Glazier Book)
The New Jerome Bible Handbook, edited with J. A. Fitzmyer and
   R. E. Murphy